SATURDAY'S CHI

TO MY FAMILY

Since I can never see your face,
And never shake you by the hand,
I send my soul through time and space
To greet you. You will understand.
James Elroy Flecker

SATURDAY'S CHILD

A Worcestershire Childhood

Wendy Grounds

Cappella Archive

Book on Demand Limited Editions

Cappella Archive
Foley Terrace · Great Malvern · England

Printed on Demand · August 1999

British Library Cataloguing-in-Publication Data
A catalogue record for this book is
available from the British Library

ISBN 1–902918–00–2

*Typeset in a Cappella realization of Fry's Baskerville of 1769
and printed on Five Seasons paper from John Purcell of London.*

iv

Saturday's Child has been accepted by the British
Library as a contribution to the Millennium Life
Story Collection. Some names have been changed
and a few incidents are modified to preserve
anonymity.

I have to thank Cora Weaver for her valuable
assistance in the preparation of the text.
W.G.

Chapter One

Late Summer 1934

THE grey stone wall divided the garden from the lane, but three quarters of the way along its length the stones had been arranged in steps to make easy access from the garden to the lane. On the steps with her knees bent up under her chin, was a scraggy child with straight brown hair, sun-tanned arms and legs, freckles across her nose and a serious face. She was watching a boy who was kicking stones in the dust at the bend of the lane. The boy's image was strangely distorted by a heat mirage which was puzzling the child for she had never seen such a thing before.

After a few minutes the boy stopped kicking, emerged out of the haze and ran towards the steps on the wall. He was wearing an old pair of flannel trousers held up with a snake clasp and a pair of braces. His shirt was collarless and his socks fell in folds over the top of his boots.

"If you look down there," said the girl, pointing down the lane, "the road's moving up and down."

The boy sat on the bottom step and glanced down the lane. Having convinced himself that the road was normal, he looked at the girl and muttered, "You're a daft thing." He then began to pull at the tufts of wild pansies that were growing in the cracks of the wall, crushing their velvety purple and gold petals.

"Jimmy Stallard, stop that," said the girl. "They are our flowers, not yours. Go away." She swung a leg towards him with annoyance.

Jimmy looked at the girl, surprised that his unconscious action should have brought forth such a protest.

"Oh, shut up you, Thea," he blurted out, "I'll pull the flowers out if I want to, you silly thing. Any road, are you going to school after the holiday?"

Thea had heard some mention of school, not that she knew what it meant or what school was, so she said, "Yes, I think so."

"Are you walking with us lot?" Jimmy enquired. "Anyhow," he added, "we mightn't let yer."

Thea ignored his remark and, turning her head, looked across the garden. The air was still and hot with the bees droning in the lavender. A plump tortoise-shell cat lay under the catmint, not curled, but stretched out because of the heat. Old Tom was digging potatoes. When he pressed his boot on the fork the thinness of his leg showed through his trousers and, when he bent to put them into the galvanized bucket, the ladder of his spine showed through his shirt.

Jimmy Stallard pulled himself up onto the wall so that he could see clearly into the garden. "He's digging his tatties too early," he said, with all the wisdom of a grown man, in his shrill seven year's old voice. "My Dad's not digging his yet. My Dad's tatties is the best anywhere, no one grows um so big."

Thea thought it was cheeky of him to sit on the wall unasked, but she didn't say anything. She was a little afraid of him for he was hard and spiky and had a habit of saying things that could hurt. Also he could punch and she hated being punched. She knew nothing about potatoes, except that they were dug out of the ground, so she didn't offer an opinion.

She looked closely at Jimmy Stallard as he pulled his socks straight, thinking how dirty his nails were, how big his ears, yet his eyes had that clear transparent blue of a marble. Yes, she had a marble in her marble bag that looked just like Jimmy Stallard's eyes.

With a stabbing suddenness Jimmy said, "Where's your mother?"

Thea looked across the garden to where an elderly woman was hanging out washing. "She's there," she said.

"No," said Jimmy impatiently, "your real Mam, where's your real Mam? She just looks after you."

"She's working," replied Thea defensively. She really didn't know what Jimmy meant but she knew she had to say something.

"Your Mammy, there," drawled Jimmy, nodding his head in the direction of the washing line, "has always brought up kids, hundreds and hundreds of kids; so my Mam says."

Thea felt hurt and uneasy, and wished Jimmy Stallard would go away. She watched Mammy struggling to get the ends of the sheets even, before pegging them on to the line. She held a number of pegs in her mouth and her grey hair fell limply because there was not a breath of wind to stir them. Mammy bent down to the washing basket and her ample backside pulled her skirt up revealing her stout black-stockinged thighs. She vigorously flapped the pillowcases, pulling them into shape, took out some more pegs from her pocket placing them in her mouth, and began to peg the pillow-cases along the line. She wore small steel-framed glasses which made her eyes seem cold and hard, giving her face an austere look. She rarely smiled so her mouth was set in a thin disgruntled line.

Monica, a fair haired little girl, younger than Thea, came round the corner of the house and went towards Mammy and the washing-basket. "I help, I help," she shrieked, her excited baby voice pulsating across the garden.

"Careful, careful." Mammy's voice was stern. "Don't you drop the things in the dirt or I'll tan you."

The child stood, a garment in either hand, waiting for Mammy to take them. She seemed unconcerned about any threat of tanning and chatted away merrily.

The sound of the voice had attracted Tom's attention and he stood up from his digging and looked towards her, rubbing his back momentarily with his hands. He smiled at the sight of the little figure, tummy sticking out through her blue cotton frock, sun-bonnet hanging by its ribbon down her back, and sturdy brown legs without socks. He leaned against his fork and took a tobacco roll from his trouser pocket and filled his pipe. He lit a match and sucked the stem of his pipe and as he did so his cheeks became hollows in his gaunt face. A pale curl of smoke twisted from the pipe drifting grey round his face. He leaned more heavily on the fork and pushed his cap towards the back of his head.

A boy came down the lane on an old bicycle, his hands on his head, trying to see how far he could go without touching the handlebars. When he saw Jimmy Stallard on the wall he quickly held the handlebars and applied the brakes. The bicycle came to a skidding halt, throwing up the dust.

"Are yer coming Jim?" he shouted. "I'll gi yer a ride if yer wants, down the hill to Bluebell Bottom."

Jimmy Stallard was off the wall in a shot, leaping on to the cross-bar of the bicycle, and the two young boys, in a pother of dust and heat haze, disappeared down the lane, round the bend and out of sight.

Thea got down from the wall and walked up the garden path towards the cottage. When she got to the catmint she bent down rubbing her face into the warm fur of the tortoise-shell cat. She loved to feel the cat's fur on her face and to smell the delicate animal fragrance which was a mixture of mint, dried grasses and earth. The cat began to purr, its body trembling through her face with the sound in her ear like the waterfall at a mill-race. After giving the cat two loud kisses on the head, she left it and walked on up the path.

"I told you not to kiss the dirty thing," Tom shouted, "you'll get worms." Thea didn't make a reply, but she thought to herself that she didn't care if she did get worms; she loved the cat and anyhow it would be rather nice to have worms; then she and the cat could sleep together in the dairy.

She watched Mammy and Monica go in through the doorway of the cottage into the big sunlit sitting room, so she pushed open the door of the dairy, which was on the side of the cottage away from the sun. It was no longer a dairy but was now an all-purpose room, used for washing and storing things. Marjory was in the dairy, putting fruit from a large black saucepan into a muslin bag.

"What are you doing, Marg?" Thea enquired, going up close to the older girl and leaning against her arm.

"Making jelly for Mam," Marjory replied. The fruit splashed on to her face and made spots down the front of her pinafore.

"Move away, Thea," Marjory said, "otherwise you'll get covered in the stuff and the stains don't come out." Thea moved to the other side of the old iron pump and sat on a cider barrel. The metal rings struck cold on her bare legs. She thought how clever Marjory was to be able to make jelly; she wished she could have a go at making jelly.

Marjory was a tall, slender girl of around thirteen, her hair, though thin and straggly, was a pretty, fair colour with a hint of auburn.

"Have I got a real mother, Marg?" Thea enquired. "I mean a mother as well as Mammy?"

"Of course you 'ave, silly, why do you ask?" Marjory replied.

Again Thea felt afraid and defensive. "I just wondered," she said.

"She comes," said Marjory, "you know she comes."

"Who?" said Thea. "Who comes? I don't know."

Marjory hoisted the muslin bag up on to a hook, placing a large bowl under it to catch the juice. She looked at Thea with a puzzled expression as though she couldn't believe that the child could be so silly. "Mabel comes. Your Mum, Mabel, comes. You know who she is, your Mum, Mabel?"

Thea kicked her legs against the barrel and watched Marjory adjusting the muslin bag to the bowl. The juice dropped down with rapid, violent, red plops. A feeling of bewilderment and disappointment swept through her. Mabel, yes she knew Mabel, but Mabel took little notice of her. She seemed much fonder of Laurence, Vincent and baby Monica.

"Have you got a mother, Marg?" Thea asked. "Apart from Mam, I mean."

Marjory shook her head. "No, my mother is dead. Mammy's got me on a permanent foster until I go out to work next year, or to live with me Gran." What a permanent foster was Thea couldn't imagine, but she really couldn't see any point in Mabel being her mother if Mabel didn't like her.

Marjory moved the handle of the pump up and down about eight times until a clear spout of water tumbled into the stone sink. "Come on, Thea, pump the water for me, then I can wash myself proper," Marjory called.

Thea jumped down from the barrel, scratching her leg as she did so on a sharp part of the barrel's rim, and walked over to the pump. Marjory's hands were stained red with the juice from the currants so she put them under the spout of the water, rubbing a lump of yellow soap into them at the same time.

"Have I always been here, Marg?" Thea blurted out, almost breathless from the effort of pumping the handle up and down.

"No, dafty, you've only been here a year. Can't you remember coming? Mabel brought you here after you had not been very well. You used to live with some people called Brown, in Birmingham, and Mabel thought the country air would be better for you—after you nearly died—and that." Marjory paused, drying her hands on an old piece of towelling. "You were here though as a little baby. Mam looked after you when you were very little and then Mabel took you away to be nearer to her."

Thea sat down on the stone flags of the dairy and picked up a bag of marbles she had left in the corner. She tipped them out into her lap, putting her hands amongst them, feeling their comforting roundness. She tried hard to think of Mabel, the Browns in Birmingham and the importance of what Marjory had just said.

Marjory gave her face a final rub with the towel and went out of the dairy, leaving the door open. Thea looked into the garden. It was all so familiar to her, every tree, every bush, every flower; surely she had been here for ever and ever, every minute of her old five years. It seemed funny to hear Marjory say that she hadn't always been here. Thea picked up the marble that looked like Jimmy Stallard's eyes and rolled it across the floor. It rolled along and stopped in one of the grooves between the flags winking back at her tauntingly.

"Jimmy Stallard's got a Mum," whispered Thea to herself. "Jimmy Stallard's got a Mum and Dad, and a sister."

As she thought, she began to recall Mrs Brown, the house and all the children. She remembered being alone in the dark, and being ill, afraid and hurt. Suddenly she felt unhappy and wanted the cat. She wanted to love and hold the cat; to hold the cat close against her face to stop the thoughts coming into her mind. She put the marbles back into the hessian bag deciding that she would go back into the garden to seek the comfort of the cat, when Tom, with little Monica close at his heels, entered the dairy.

Tom was carrying two buckets of potatoes which he put down heavily on the stone floor. He spread a sack on the floor, placed a sieve on the sack and tipped one of the buckets of potatoes into the sieve. Monica, kneeling on the floor, started to play with the potatoes, rubbing the dirt off with her chubby little hands.

Tom swilled out the bucket at the pump until all the mud had gone, and then refilled the bucket with clear, cold water. Taking off his cap and shirt, he tucked his braces into the waist of his trousers and began to wash himself vigorously in the bucket. Monica, picking up a wooden box, struggled over to the sink with it, pulled herself on to it, so that she could stand by the side of Tom with her arms in the bucket of water.

Thea walked towards the sink, which was under the window, to watch Tom washing while Monica laughingly spilt his water. The water splashed on to the stone flags, trickling between the cracks in the stones. Thea kept her distance as she didn't want to get wet but she was drawn towards the warmth and gaiety that flowed between Tom and the little girl. He had infinite patience with her, rarely getting cross, however naughty her ways. It was a known fact that old Tom loved the baby, but he was never openly or intentionally unkind to any of the children. He would sometimes shout at them, but he was never unkind. Mammy, on the other hand, could get very angry, lashing out with her big, red hands, striking any part of anyone's body that happened to be in the direct line of fire at that particular moment.

Mammy and Tom frequently argued and sometimes came to blows. It was usually Mammy that got angry with something that Tom had or hadn't done and she would shout loudly and even throw things. Thea hated it when Mammy threw things, so she would run to the bottom of the orchard to sit in the ditch. If it was dark when the fighting began, she would sit in the grate inside the fender, for Mammy never threw things in the direction of the grate because her favourite objects, such as bits of china, were arranged on the mantelpiece. Marjory would run upstairs, Monica would cry hysterically and the boys, Laurence and Vincent, would shout at the two adults to stop fighting, even attempting to intervene.

Tom tipped the bucket of water down the sink and began to dry himself vigorously on the old towel which had been thrown over the chair by Marjory. He stopped for a moment and dried Monica's arms and the front of her dress.

"Are you going to shave, Tom? Can I help you shave?" The baby voice echoed round the dairy.

"Yes, Tom must shave, make himself look smart to go into Worcester. I'm catching the twenty past two bus, so I must hurry," said Tom. He went to the dairy door and called loudly to Laurence and enquired whether he was going with him on the bus to Worcester and told him, if he was, to come in and get ready.

Laurence was at the far end of the orchard with a group of boys playing some sort of game with a ball and a bat.

"Thea, be a good little lass and go down and tell Laurence I want him," said Tom. "I must get on and do my shaving or I'll miss the bus."

Thea placed the bag of marbles behind one of the geranium pots on the window sill and ran out of the dairy into the orchard. She didn't take her marbles because the boys would only want to pinch them and she didn't want that to happen. Running down through the orchard Thea shouted and waved her arms.

"Laurie, Laurie, Tom wants you. He says go and talk to him. He's shaving." Thea was quite breathless when she reached the group of boys. "Laurie, Tom wants you," she puffed. "He wants you to go to Worcester with him."

Laurence was a tall, fair-haired, good-looking boy, a year or so younger than Marjory. He had strong muscular shoulders and brown, straight legs. He ignored Thea and shouted to a smaller, red-haired, freckled face boy to give him one more bowl. "Come on Vince, give it all you can. I'll swipe it right down across the ditch, then I'll have to go, I suppose, 'cause Tom's waiting."

The smaller boy ran, bowled, and Laurence hit the ball majestically making it zoom through the air with such speed that Thea lost sight of it as it disappeared over the trees at the far end of the orchard. Laurence threw down the bat and made his way back to the house, while several boys ran in the direction of the ball in the hope of finding it.

Laurence and Vincent lived with Mammy and Tom, but the other boys had come from London for a few weeks. Thea didn't know where London was, but all she knew was that the group of boys were called 'the London boys' and that they were somewhat different. They slept in the attic on mattresses which were placed in rows on the floor. They were each given a pillow and a grey blanket to cover them, and they had to wash at the pump in the garden. They ate separately and sometimes went up to the farm to give a hand. The rest of the time they played around the orchard or fields, or helped in the garden or the house if asked to. Thea liked the way they talked and they were always gentle with her, although they often quarrelled among themselves.

Thea sat down under one of the gnarled apple trees and leaned against the rough lichen covered trunk. Alfie, one of the London boys, came to sit beside her. His big toenail protruded through a hole in his black pump and his legs were covered in scratches and bruises.

"What's London like?" Thea asked suddenly.

"Oh, just a place, a big dirty place, with lots of smoke, factories, lorries and noise. Well, where I live it is anyway," said Alfie cheerily. "Anyhow, I likes it, I likes it better than this country. I don't really like this country and cows and fings." Alfie spoke in a sharp, clipped way, never sounding his ts and cutting the ends off each word. He had a cheerful confidence about him as though he knew he was going to do all right in life.

Thea, uncertain of what to say, said, "I like cows, and I specially like hens."

"Like hens?" exclaimed Alfie in disbelief. "I fink them's silly fings, I do, and I don't like it when her," he pointed his thumb in the direction of the cottage, "when her makes me clean 'em out."

"They've got fleas, little red fleas," said Thea with sudden happiness in her voice, "and the fleas get all over you." She waited to see what effect her knowledge of the hen mite would have on Alfie.

Alfie chewed a piece of grass and thoughtfully picked at a scab on his knee. "We've got fleas all over the place in London," he said with a certain amount of pride in his voice. "And," he added conspiratorially, "we've got bed bugs."

From the tone in Alfie's voice Thea gathered that bed bugs were something very special, so not wanting to be outdone, she said, "Our cat's got worms."

This last statement was ignored by Alfie as he saw the boys coming back up through the orchard, and he wanted to bat. He got up, grabbed Laurie's bat and stood expectantly waiting for someone to bowl.

She thought she would go back into the garden, as it was no good wanting to play with the boys. The bat was so big that she could never swing it and the ball hurt when it hit her legs. Anyhow on a Saturday afternoon Monica's mother always visited and Monica's mother was full of fun. Thea loved the way she shrieked with laughter over everything. Mammy always seemed happy when Monica's mother was around.

Monica's mother rode a bicycle and usually had lots of things in the basket fixed to the handlebars. She had a seat fixed to the back of the bicycle where she placed Monica when she took her for a ride. Thea thought how lucky Monica was. She wasn't jealous of Monica, but sometimes wished she was Monica, and could be the baby, have golden curls and be kissed by a mother called Stella, who always laughed.

She walked up through the orchard and, as she did so, kicked the large clumps of stinging nettles that were grouped under the trees. Yellow dust sprayed over her legs and down the front of her dress. Brown speckled hens were scratching here and there under the hedge and one had found a patch of bare, warm earth and was giving herself a dust bath. The hen looked at Thea, winking its bright golden eye, made a warm chortling sound in its throat, but went on spraying dust over its back feathers.

As she walked back into the garden, Stella was coming in through the gate off the lane, pushing her bicycle in front of her. Her face was red with the effort of riding in the heat and her hair was clinging to the sweat on her forehead. Stella shrieked a general greeting to anyone within earshot, at the same time calling out loudly for a cold drink of water, saying if she didn't get it she was sure she would die, as she was the hottest that she had ever been in her whole life.

Little Monica ran out through the open door leaping into her mother's arms. Mammy came to the door making noises of surprise that Stella should have ridden in such heat.

"Come on in, my dear, in the cool," she said, "and I'll get you a drink. Water or ginger beer? I thought you would have caught the bus," went on Mammy, "I didn't think you would cycle in this heat. Tom's gone into Worcester as usual with Laurie. Here, sit by the window, there's a nice current of air there. It will cool you."

Stella sat down with Monica on her knee and she took the glass of cold ginger beer from Mammy and held it against her forehead to cool herself before she drank it.

"A fortnight now this heat's been on. There'll be a storm before long, you mark my words, such a storm. I hope they get the harvest in, though, before it breaks." She kissed Monica several times and hugged her close to her, telling her that she was her darling, her best, her sweetest.

The room was reasonably cool and shady except for one rich, golden sandwich of sunlight that cut from the doorway across the stone floor, coming to rest on the old dresser than ran along the wall adjoining the dairy. Dust danced in the sunlight and dust lay thickly underneath the dresser. On the dresser were crammed objects accumulated over the years. It's doubtful whether some of the things had been moved for ten years or more. There were books, odd pieces of china, broken necklaces, scissors, a hammer, a screw-driver, two large vegetable dishes and a number of meat dishes. Apart from the dresser the room contained a large table with a scrubbed top and stout legs, plus a variety of chairs, such as elm ladder-backs, oak Windsors, rush-seated chairs and cane chairs, all looking somewhat knocked about with the continual usage. There was also in the room a black leather and horsehair sofa, and two wooden grandfather chairs on either side of the iron range.

Thea lay in the patch of sunlight on the stone floor, playing with a celluloid wind-up toy. The toy was a doll which pushed a pram and it would move across the floor a few inches coming to a halt every time it reached an uneven join in the stone flags. Although she enjoyed the conversation of the two women, their voices flow-ing over her in warm waves, she decided to take the toy out on to the garden path to see how far it would go with each wind-up. It had been a birthday present given her the week before. Coming down to breakfast one morning Mammy had handed her a parcel.

"It's your birthday, Thea," she said, "you're five now. Here's a present for you. It's come in the post."

She didn't know who had sent the present but inside the parcel were two books and the wind-up toy. Marjory had read her one of the stories from the book and she had liked looking at the pictures. The one book was about a duck that danced, splashing mud every-where, and the other book was something to do with a bear. Thea was not acquainted with birthdays and they held no place of importance in her mind. Apart from the parcel in the morning no other mention of birthday was made until tea time, when it was unanimously agreed by everyone round the tea table that she should have the last piece of fruit cake, because it was her birthday. She ate this last piece of cake with a sort of honoured reverence, puzzling in her mind what a birthday was.

The celluloid toy was beginning to trundle nicely along the stone path when Thea's attention was diverted by the slamming of a car door. Not many cars were seen in the lane so she stopped playing and looked over the garden wall in time to see a large black car moving off and Mabel coming in through the garden gate. Mabel was wearing a navy–blue silk dress with a white pointed collar and she wore very high–heeled shoes. She tottered in through the gate carrying a large brown parcel.

"Hello, Thea," she called, "you'd better come and see what I've got in this box for you." She walked past the child and in through the cottage door greeting the two women in the sitting room with, "Surprise, surprise, you didn't expect to see me, darlings, did you? I've been brought by car and will be picked up again in two hours."

Thea stood against the hollyhocks, that were growing by the garden wall, clutching the celluloid toy. Mabel was her mother, so Marjory had said, so Mabel now was something quite different. Mabel didn't kiss her or pat her head or cuddle her, but she had walked past her with a big, big box that she said was for her.

Thea felt confused and embarrassed and didn't want to go into the sitting room, even though a pulling curiosity was drawing her that way. She could hear Mabel's loud, clear voice echoing out through the door and Stella's shrill laughter responding to her remarks.

Marjory appeared at the bend in the lane coming from the direction of the farm, carrying in her arms a large basket full of eggs, and straight away Thea relaxed. She didn't mind going indoors if she could go in with Marjory. She ran along opening the garden gate for Marjory, who explained to Thea that she was going to wash and sort the eggs for Mrs Tarrent, the farmer's wife.

"Stella's here," said Thea quietly, "and Mabel. She came in a black car and she's got a box with her."

"I 'spect it's your birthday present." replied the older girl, in a matter–of–fact voice. "She's bound to have brought you a birthday present, after all it was your birthday last week."

The two girls entered the living room and Marjory placed the basket of eggs carefully on the table amongst the cups and saucers which had been spread out ready for tea. Mammy suggested that a more suitable place should be found for the eggs, so Marjory said that she would take them into the dairy where she would wash them.

"Well," said Stella, suddenly looking to where Thea was standing by the table, "little Thea is five, what about that Mabel?" She smiled at the child, adding, "Such a big girl, soon to be going to school."

"She is ready for school. She'll like school," said Mabel author-
itatively. "Now, shall we see what is in the parcel? This is to do with
school."

Thea felt from the tone in Mabel's voice that the contents of the
box were to do with school rather than with her, but, however, she
was interested just in case there was something inside like a doll or a
box of paints. As the string was untied all sorts of delicious fantasies
began to float through her mind and she became very excited.

Monica, climbing on to a chair, began to help with the untying of
the string and when the brown paper was folded back she laughed
excitedly. Thea stood by the table watching, her cheeks burning in
dreadful anticipation.

Vincent and a few of the boys had come into the garden from the
orchard and they could be heard washing their hands under the
pump that was by the orchard gate. Thea hoped that they would
stay in the garden as she wanted to savour the contents of the box
without their presence. They were pushing each other under the
spout with loud bellows and shouts. Mammy shouted at them to
stop wasting water because, with all the hot weather, the well would
dry up and then where would they be?

The string was off the box, then the brown paper and at last the
lid was opened revealing what appeared to be a black rug.

"Now come here. Thea," shrilled Mabel, "come and see if you
don't think this is lovely and just the thing for school. You will be
smart, mark my word, you will be smart." She shook the black
object and held it out in front of Thea.

It was a coat, a black woollen coat. Undoing the buttons, she held
it out for Thea to put on. Thea's thin arms slipped into the silk
lining of the sleeves but the coat hung heavily on her narrow shoulders. She couldn't see her hands but she could feel the woollen edge
of the coat rough below her knees.

Mabel put her hand across the shoulders. "That's fine," she said.
"Room there for growth and winter woollies. Now the hat, let us
look at the hat."

From the box she took out a black velour hat, placing it on Thea's
head. At this moment Vincent came to the door and he let out a
great shriek of laughter, which attracted the attention of two of the
boys who were frolicking by the pump so that they ran over to the

door to see what the laughter was about.

"Look at old Thea. Doesn't she look a twit; she looks like a crow," Vincent hooted, leaning against the door post, holding his stomach in laughter.

"She looks very grown up," said Mabel, "a real schoolgirl."

"Clear off," Mammy shouted at the door, "clear off you boys and stop being stupid."

"It's too hot," said Thea feebly, with tears smarting her eyes. "It's too hot today."

"Of course it is," soothed Stella, "but it will be lovely when it's cold and you've got to walk all that way to school in the snow."

As far as Thea was concerned it had always been hot and, as for snow, she couldn't remember ever having seen snow. All she could think of was how pleased she would be when the coat was taken off and put back into the box. There were no pretty shoes or ribbons, just a black coat, a thick, black coat for a birthday present.

Stella, sensing the waves of misery coming from the little figure encased in the black hat and coat, took the velour hat off the child's head and placed it among the cups and saucers. "Come on," she said in a jolly voice. "I've got some bon-bons. I know you like bon-bons." She started to undo the buttons on the coat.

"I know it seems big," exclaimed Mabel, "but they do grow at this age and it should last two winters."

Mammy eyed the velour hat with a look of grave misgiving. "I think a beret would have been more sensible. That hat'll get knocked about at school, trodden on and ruined."

Stella took Thea's hand and led her outside to the bicycle and the sweets, while Mabel stroked the velour hat defensively. Monica trotted out after her mother and Thea. Mammy, lifting the steaming kettle from the range, filled the earthenware teapot that was sitting expectantly on the hob.

"I don't like that coat," said Thea.

Stella gave a small, tight laugh of forced jollity. "It will keep out the cold, my duck—it will be fine." She squeezed Thea's hand. "I've got something for you in my saddle bag, something to make you look very special."

She let go of the small hand wishing desperately that she had bought something extra for the child. The ribbons she had were really for Monica, but she would give them to Thea for the child had so little. "There you are," she said handing the light package to Thea and taking out the bags of bon-bons.

The child held the tissue paper in her hand embarrassed and afraid to open it.

"What is it, what is it?" piped Monica.

"Let Thea undo it," whispered Stella. "Come on my chicken, look inside."

Thea folded back the paper and saw the yellow satin ribbons. A faint smile spread across her face and a lump rose in Stella's throat. She hated Mabel for being so insensitive. How could a little girl of five like a thick black coat, and ugly velour hat?

"Come here and I'll tie them in your hair," she said, handing the bags of sweets to Monica and pulling the child towards her. Taking a comb from the pocket of her dress she pulled the straight brown hair back from the child's face and tied it up in a large yellow bow on top of her head.

"There you are my duck, don't you look really lovely."

Thea didn't know what she looked like, but if Stella said she looked lovely, then she must do. She stood by the bicycle smiling self consciously at Stella. Suddenly finding her tongue she said, "Why is Mabel my mother? Who made her my mother?"

Momentarily Stella was thrown by the strangeness of the question, but she knew what the child meant, because on the few occasions she had seen Mabel with her daughter, there had been no affection, no warmth. Mabel appeared to visit Hacketts Cottage out of duty, longing to get away at the earliest opportunity. Not that she really knew Mabel; it was just that their children were being fostered by the same person. She gave the child a little hug; "It's just that she is, my duck. She is your mother; you were her baby."

Thea mulled the words over in her mind, 'you were her baby,' while Monica stuffed a bon-bon in her mouth and handed one to Thea. She had never imagined herself being a baby, let alone Mabel's baby. She couldn't imagine herself being anything other than she was now.

"Come on," trilled Stella cheerfully. "Let's go and show them the ribbons."

In the mellow heat of the early evening Marjory put Thea and Monica to bed. Mabel had gone in a flurry of excitement when a car arrived to pick her up. Stella left on her bicycle after helping Mammy to wash up the tea things. Great piles of cups and plates had lain in the stone sink of the dairy following the boys' hungry assault on the plates of bread and butter and home-made jam.

Thea lay in bed with Monica asleep by her side, watching the patches of evening sunlight glowing on the ceiling and listening to the raucous shouts of the boys at play in the garden. It was a spacious room with a sloping ceiling, containing a black iron bedstead, where Mammy and Tom slept, and several large wardrobes and a chest of drawers. Thea's mind was a confused jigsaw of images, thoughts and notions. The black hat, the coat, school, birthday and Mabel were all mixed up. To go to school you had to be five, and the black coat and hat were a necessary part of going to school and they had to be brought by Mabel because Mabel was her mother, and in some way it was a present and she was meant to be pleased.

A thick fear swept through her body. If she had to wear that hat and coat to school the boys would laugh at her every day and call her a crow and knock her hat off and kick it in the mud. Tears filled her eyes and she wiped them away on the edge of the sheet. She wondered what school was like and why everyone went to school and, what is more, what they did at school. Jimmy Stallard and his lot, she was sure, must do dreadful things at school.

Pushing out of her mind the distasteful thought of school, boys and black coats, Thea began to think of Mrs Brown. It was because Marjory had reminded her of Mrs Brown that made the figure emerge from the deep recesses of her mind, taking on shape and form. She remembered the voice and appearance of Mrs Brown and the living room where they had all spent so much of their time. There wasn't a Mr Brown, just a Mrs Brown and a lot of children. One of the children, a girl about Marjory's age, had called Mrs Brown Mum, but to the rest of the children she was Mrs Brown.

She remembered that Mrs Brown was tall and thin with fluffy brown hair, brown eyes and a brown frock, which was why, she decided, she was called Mrs Brown. Mrs Brown was always shouting and the children were always noisy. Thea was the youngest of the children and the only one who didn't go to school, so every school day a great calm descended on the house. Thea was left much to herself while Mrs Brown spent most of the time washing, ironing, scrubbing and cooking. When the children returned from school noise and chaos returned too and the dreadful shouting began.

Although she hadn't liked the noise and roughness of the other children, neither had she liked being left alone in the dark. Mrs Brown would put her to bed, for a little nap she called it, and then would go out. She lay in bed in the silent house, watching the branches of the trees moving across the window or watching the raindrops trickling down the glass. Her memory was of the winter afternoons when it would begin to get dark early and how horrible it was when the room began to get gloomier and gloomier until there was no light left at all.

One afternoon, when completely enveloped in the ear-splitting, silent blackness, she got out of bed and made her way to the stairs. She felt for the top of the first stair and began to wriggle her bottom down to the next, then the next, and so on until reaching the end. There was a door at the bottom of the stairs which went into the living room, but she couldn't reach the latch for it was too high.

She banged on the door, crying out, but the house only answered back in a mocking silence. She had stayed huddled there weeping and afraid for what seemed to her to be hours. She was afraid to go back up the stairs, so lay trapped in a tunnel of darkness filled with all manner of unimaginable horrible things.

Mrs Brown returned together with the children from school. Someone opened the stair door causing Thea to roll into the living room. Mrs Brown was lighting the gas mantle at the time and she was startled by the sudden emergence of the little sobbing body.

"What the devil are you doing there?" she exclaimed. "I left you for your nap. Why didn't you stay where I left you, you naughty girl?" She dragged Thea to her feet and gave her a hard slap across the shoulders. "When I put you upstairs, my lady, you stay there. Do you understand? Don't you dare do that again." She got the poker and began to rake the fire vigorously. "Now the damn thing's gone out," she whined. "Trevor, go into the yard and get me some sticks. I shall have to relight it."

Thea didn't mind about the slap or the noise or the fire going out;

she was just pleased to be in the light again and to hear voices.

A young woman called Daisy, who called Mrs Brown Mum, used to visit some afternoons. She had a daughter, younger than Thea, who called Mrs Brown Nana. The two women would chat over tea and the child would toddle about playing. Thea's memory of the little girl was that she was nearly always sucking an orange that had been cut in half and, as she sucked it, the juice would trickle down her chin, up her little fat arms and drip off the point of her elbow. It was with horror that she thought of the sticky juice, the pungent smell of the orange and her overwhelming desire to keep away from the child.

She had few toys, but did possess a small tin doll's pram in which lay her much-loved teddy bear. One afternoon, the little girl, covered in sticky orange juice as usual, wanted to play with the pram and its precious occupant. As she put her hands on the handle, Thea pushed the child away making her fall over and bang her head on the sideboard. Mrs Brown and Daisy had reacted instantly, leaping to the toddler's defence. Thea had been slapped soundly and sent to bed, while the sticky little girl had been allowed to play with the doll's pram.

She rubbed her hands together under the sheets sensing so clearly the stickiness and horribleness of it all. She wasn't capable of analyzing her motives for behaving as she did, but was aware of injustices and was often amazed by the way that grown-up people behaved. She remembered going into hospital, although not knowing why she went into the place or being given any prior warning. The vast, strange building and the people dressed in white who kept dashing about came clearly to her. A mask was pressed on her face and, when she protested at the indignity of being smothered, was told not to be naughty but to lie still. She had been furious at being called naughty, as it was the grown-ups who were being naughty, so she kicked violently and then knew no more.

Quite clearly she could visualise in her mind the hospital ward and the white iron cot in which she lay. She had felt sore all over and disinclined to drink or sit up or speak. She had a faint memory of people leaning over the cot, talking or washing her or changing the sheets. She didn't know how long she she had been there or even at what point she began to feel better, but she remembered being fed jelly one day and being allowed to smell the freesias that were sitting in a vase on the locker by the side of the cot. Mabel dressed her on the day she left hospital and she recalled the surprise she felt when Mabel turned up with her clothes.

She had left the hospital by car with a man driving and Mabel sitting by his side. The streets had been busy and she felt sick and dizzy sitting in the back of the car. Mabel told the man that the doctor had said that Thea would be years getting over the illness and that she would possibly be twelve before she was really fit again.

She supposed, as she tossed in the bed next to the sleeping Monica, that that was when she came to be with Mammy. She smoothed her pillow, pulled the sheet up round her neck and went to sleep.

Chapter Two

ONE early morning in late summer, Thea found herself being propelled along the lanes by an assorted mixture of boys and girls, all heading excitedly towards the place called 'school'. It was the first day of the Autumn Term and the children refreshed by their August holiday seemed pleased to be going back into the friendly, chalky warmth of the classrooms. Thea, having no conception of where she was going, felt a certain pride at belonging to the gang of children who were part of this unknown place, but at the same time her mouth was dry with fear. She wore a cotton dress and carried her sandwiches in a satchel across her back, which bumped up and down in an unaccustomed manner as she hurried along. She held tightly to the hand of Joan Stallard, the sister of Jimmy, who had been given particular instructions to look after her.

Marjory and Laurie went to school in Worcester so they had caught an early bus. Vincent was with the group that Thea walked with, but he chased ahead with three or four other boys, throwing stones and making a lot of noise. A warm haze hung over the fields promising a hot, fine day. Men were out harnessing the horses to the reapers, or turning over the second crop of hay. The air was pungent with the sweetness of the ripe grain.

With a good deal of noise and confusion the 'London Boys' departed in a charabanc the evening before. A man came to collect them and check their things, and a general air of cheerful bonhomie pervaded the atmosphere. Everyone was out on the garden wall to wish them goodbye, even neighbours were drawn to their gates to watch the charabanc back its way down the lane.

Laurie, jumping up and down on the wall, waved his arms and shouted, "See you next year, unless I come up to 'the smoke' before that and see you."

Mammy managed to smile at the disappearing faces pressed against the bus window after telling Laurie not to be silly, and to ask him where in the world did he think he was going to get money from to go to London.

When they went back into the cottage all seemed strangely quiet for a while until Mammy began to organize the bathing. She had already got the boiler alight in the dairy and two large black kettles were steaming on the grate. The long tin bath was filled with water, some hot, some cold, and the rigmarole of the bathing begun. Monica and Thea were bathed first. Mammy knelt on the stone floor washing them vigorously with a large tablet of carbolic soap. She washed their hair with the same soap, then instructed Marjory to carry in jugs of clear water from the dairy with which to do the swilling. Marjory and Mammy dried the little girls, rubbing them on big, rough towels. Protesting loudly, Vincent was told to get undressed and get in the girls' water. After a lot of back-chat he finally took his clothes off and submitted his body to the carbolic suds.

Laurence and Marjory had clean water, but they didn't bath until the younger children were in bed. It was their job to struggle out into the garden with the tin bath and empty its contents on to the flower beds. The bathing procedure would have been going on in all the cottage homes in preparation for school, so that on the first morning of term a sweet-smelling crowd assembled.

The school was positioned about a mile and a half from the village, but it was central to a number of villages or hamlets, so children poured into the school from all directions. Thea couldn't believe her eyes for she had never before seen so many children all at once. They seemed to fill the playground and the noise was incredibly loud. Joan Stallard had pushed her in through the school gate, then promptly disappeared in search of her friend.

Anchorless and terrified, Thea stood rooted among the alien crowd. Every child seemed to be laughing and shouting with others and there was a great deal of rushing about, pushing and jostling. From her island of misery Thea watched the frenzied activity, contemplating the awfulness of the situation if Joan did not return.

Suddenly the large door of the building opened and a lady with flaming red hair appeared, ringing a hand bell with strident clangour. The shouting suddenly stopped and every child became a statue. A piercing whistle rent the air which told the children to move again quickly and get into lines.

Joan Stallard rushed up to Thea, grabbed her by the arm and pushed her along into one of the lines. "When Miss calls your line, you go in," she hissed. "Do as Miss says, or you'll get the cane."

"Little ones in first," shrilled the lady with the flaming hair. "New ones stand by the desk."

Thea's line moved and she followed. She looked round despairingly for Joan, but she was nowhere in sight. The line moved into the classroom and standing by the door was a lady with soft grey hair and a gentle face. She smiled sweetly, ushering the children in.

"I wants me Mam," a small voice shouted, choked with tears. "I wants to go 'ome to me Mam."

"Come along," soothed the lady with the gentle face, "we've got eight new ones this morning, you aren't on your own. Your mother will be waiting for you after school."

The small boy was not convinced for he was in a state of abject terror so he gave further vent to his feelings by howling even louder. The gentle-faced teacher, used to many decades of sobbing, first-day children, went to the piano and began to play.

"Come along, round the piano," she called. "We will all sing 'All Things Bright and Beautiful'. Let me see if you have still got your voices after the long summer holiday." She put her hands on the keyboard, and out floated, what to Thea, was a most magical sound.

The children who had been in school before began to sing. The sobbing child stopped his noise, and the new ones, Thea included, stood transfixed. The teacher had a loud, clear voice, and the children sang pipingly shrill. When a few verses had been sung Thea learnt the chorus so she joined in with the rest, feeling very grown up and important.

When the singing was over, the teacher stood up from the piano and said, "Let us pray." Everyone shut their eyes and placed their hands together. Thea partly closed her eyes, peeping through her fingers to see what was going on. The teacher prayed for our Father Arthur in heaven, Harold be thy name, and Thea was really puzzled why these men were prayed for, and in fact continued to be prayed for day after day.

The teacher then allotted seats to everyone, which seemed to cause a considerable amount of excitement and consternation. Thea sat down where she was told and gazed round at the interesting paraphernalia of the schoolroom. The teacher began to call the children's names from a list that she had in front of her. The children answered, "Present, Miss Thomas", which Thea thought was very strange, Miss Thomas could obviously see that for herself that they were all present.

A little girl called Topsy was put in the seat next to Thea. She had long golden ringlets that fell in rigid individual twirls on to her shoulder, and bright pink cheeks like nicely polished apples, and fat arms.

Miss Thomas placed the eight infants near to one another, giving each of them a tray containing sand, and instructed them to trace a big round *a* with their finger in the sand. They were to keep on doing this until their *a* was as round and lovely as the one she had drawn on the board with chalk. She then went to another group and gave them slates, and gave books to some others.

The room began to resound with the scratching sound of slate pencils mixed with the murmur of voices saying, "Kitty runs after the ball. Rover runs after the ball. Mother runs after Rover. Rover runs after Kitty. Kitty runs up the tree." Over the sound of the murmuring and the scratching and the giggling from the infants was Miss Thomas's soft voice, advising, encouraging and guiding.

The sunlight poured through the large windows, and the roses in a copper bowl on the teacher's desk were reflected in the first day of term polish.

Thea rubbed her finger in the sand tray and looked up at the picture in front of her. It was of a sad looking man tied on to a piece of wood, with blood trickling from his feet and hands. Spiky thorns were round his head and blood was pouring down his face. The man had such sad eyes and Thea wondered what he had to do with the schoolroom.

"Why is the poor man being hurt?" Thea asked Miss Thomas. "Who has nailed him to the wood?"

"Ah," replied Miss Thomas with a sad expression, "that is Our Lord. He died for our sins, so that we should be saved. Think of that dear child, He died for us all."

Thea thought and thought, but she couldn't ever remember having seen the poor man. She couldn't imagine why he was nailed like that on to the wood, unless someone had been naughty.

"He is with you always," soothed Miss Thomas. "He sees everything you do and He cares for you. He is even in bed with you at night."

A shock wave of surprise went through Thea's body, for she was sure he wasn't in bed with her and Monica. Anyhow, how could he be, for he was hanging on the classroom wall. "Did you say in bed, Miss?" ventured Thea feebly, hoping that she had misheard Miss Thomas.

"He is with you always my dear," said Miss Thomas gently. "He never leaves you. If you love Him He will always take care of you."

Thea felt afraid and worried, so she took her eyes off the picture and traced a big round *a* in her sand tray.

Topsy was twirling the sand round in her sand tray at an alarming rate and some of it was cascading out over the desk. She chuckled to herself, making her stiff ringlets bob up and down. Thea was sure Miss Thomas was mistaken, for how could the poor, hurt man in the picture be in bed with her? She didn't mind him sharing the bed but she couldn't see how it could happen.

Thea was fascinated by Topsy's ringlets, so she caught hold of one to see what it felt like, but at that moment Topsy turned her head in the opposite direction causing the hair to be pulled sharply. With a shriek of surprise and indignation Topsy swung round and grabbed Thea's cheek, pinching it with her fat little fingers. Thea's shriek was equally as loud as Topsy's and by the time Miss Thomas was at their side they were both howling loudly. Topsy's sand tray was on the floor and the small boy who had been tearful earlier let vent to his feelings and sobbed noisily.

The door opened and the teacher with the flaming red hair stood there and called, "Do you want any help, Miss Thomas? Shall I send one of the older girls in?"

"Wallop 'em, Miss," shouted a know-all from the back of the room. "That's what they wants, a good wallop, that'll shut 'em up."

"Thank you, that would be nice, Miss Greaves," a rather fraught Miss Thomas replied and then, looking at the back of the class, she told the young boy who was full of sound advice to kindly keep his thoughts to himself and his mouth closed.

The situation was calmed with the help of an older girl, and Miss Thomas's quiet manner. Crayons and paper were quickly given out in place of the sand trays and happy activity was resumed.

At midday everyone ate sandwiches, after which they were released on to the school meadow to fling themselves freely around, to exercise cramped limbs and to bring back to life voices that had been silenced for a couple of hours.

The timid boy whose name was Mervyn clung to Thea's dress and together they faced the hostile mob. Sitting on the trunk of a fallen tree, they watched in awed silence.

A bigger boy from their class suddenly spotted them and he ran up and shouted, "Sissy, sissy, Mervyn is a sissy. He cries for his Mammy." Attracted by his shouting, other children joined him until the tree trunk was surrounded by chanting children all shouting, "Mervyn is a sissy." The two infants sat marooned on the trunk and, as tears began to roll down Thea's cheeks, the chanting changed to, "Thea is a baby and Mervyn is a sissy. Thea is a baby."

Wretched, abandoned and blinded by tears, Thea clung to the trunk, while against her ear the terrified Mervyn screamed. Together they struggled in the whirlpool of misery, seeing no way of escape. Joan Stallard eventually released them. Being twelve, large and forceful, she quickly dispersed the crowd with a few clouts to the ear and some well-aimed kicks. Then, with all the protectiveness of a mother cat, she dried their tears and took them for a walk to the top part of the meadow.

The top of the meadow was yellow with dandelions and a thrush sang from the top branch of a hawthorn tree. Thea felt safe again with her hand encased in Joan's comfortable, secure hand.

Thea soon grew accustomed to school and the routine it demanded. Within a few days she learnt to cope with the bullies and the louts and within a few weeks she understood Miss Thomas, knowing exactly what to do to please her. Without any obvious effort and awareness, she learnt to read and was soon recognizing the words that told the rather dull story of the orange coloured dog Rover, chasing the white ball up the orange tree with the black Kitty watching.

One day, about six weeks after Thea had started school, Joan Stallard had a heavy cold which kept her at home in bed. Mammy instructed Vincent to take care of Thea and make sure she got to school safely. With the accustomed anchor gone, Thea set off with Vincent and the other boys to school. With whoops and shouts they chased down the lane, kicking stones at each other as they went. Thea had to run to keep up with them and, as it was the first day she had worn her thick, black coat, she was very hot when she arrived at the school.

When the time came for the boys to go home, they had forgotten all about Thea, so, instead of waiting for her, they chased down the lane in pursuit of some new quarry or game. Thea got to the school gate just in time to see their disappearing forms vanishing in the distance. She began to run encased in her thick coat and further restricted by the satchel slung across her back. Even though she ran as quickly as she could, she saw no sign and heard no sound from the boys. Her hat kept slipping and her legs felt hot in her black woollen stockings. When she arrived at a fork in the lane, she couldn't remember which way to take.

In absolute panic she stood against the tree at the fork of the two ways but nothing looked familiar, there was nothing to tell her which way to go. She could see nothing but the high hedges all round her, and an awful silence.

It was a gloomy afternoon with the threat of rain in the air. The tall hedges with their hidden depths suddenly took on a threatening appearance. Thea imagined that there were strange monsters in the hedges waiting to jump out on her, so, full of dreadful misapprehension, she began to run down one of the lanes.

Arriving at a spot where the hedge spread into a copse, Thea was sure she was lost, for she couldn't ever remember seeing the group of trees before, or the dark pond that was partly hidden in their midst. She stood and looked at the gloomy water and began to cry. She couldn't decide whether to go on or go back to try the other lane, for she was sure that at any moment it would become dark making it impossible to find her way home. Unimaginable creatures lurked in the pond and in Thea's mind they took on unbelievable proportions.

A sound attracted her attention and from the gloom of the lanes appeared two figures on bicycles. When they got nearer Thea noticed that they were two ladies with baskets laden with shopping on the front of their machines. They were chatting to each other in rather breathless voices because of the effort of cycling. They stopped cycling when they were level with Thea and one of the ladies got off her bicycle, lifted the child up and placed her on the carrier at the back of the bicycle.

"It's one of the Clements kids," she said. "I think it's disgraceful letting her walk down these lanes on her own. What about if she had fallen in that pond." She got on the bicycle, wobbling a little with the unaccustomed weight on the back, and began to cycle along the lane side by side with the other woman.

Thea held her legs out to stop them bumping on the wheels, clinging at the same time to the back of the lady's tweed coat. She wondered how the lady knew who she was, but she hadn't been able to tell her about Vince and the boys because she hadn't been given the opportunity to explain.

"There's not enough care taken, if you ask me," said the lady's cycling companion. "One of these days something will happen to one of those kids." There was a tone of foreboding in her voice.

Thea hoped they were cycling in the direction of home and that she wasn't being taken to some strange place, so she was most relieved after about ten minutes to see the familiar wall surrounding Hacketts Cottage with Vince and the other boys leaning against it.

It was a golden autumn day with a fresh wind blowing the leaves like confetti over the garden and the fields. The young bullocks, in the field opposite the cottage, were running around with their tails held high with the joy of existence. A kitten belonging to the tortoise-shell cat jumped into the leaves, leapt into the air like a boneless shadow, then shot up the trunk of the plum tree. The mother cat sat, like a statue, watching, while Thea lay sprawled along the branch of an apple tree. She liked to see the kitten chasing the leaves and dashing up and down the trees but she tried to hide from her thoughts the memory of the kittens that Mammy drowned.

The tortoise-shell cat had had four kittens but three of them had been held under the water in the water butt until their small bodies had become lifeless. When Mammy had lifted them out, they had looked like pieces of dark, damp cloth. A black shadow passed across the mild October day and Thea hoped that next time the tortoise-shell cat had kittens she would go off to some secret place and hide them from Mammy. Thea and the cat would share the secret and she would steal food and take it to the cat.

As Thea was mulling over in her mind where the secret hiding place could be for the tortoise-shell cat and her kittens, a red bus came to a halt at the bottom of the lane and a lady and gentleman alighted. To Thea's surprise they made their way to the cottage. The lady, who was holding on tightly to her hat, looked vaguely familiar to Thea, but the man was a complete stranger. She lost sight of them as they walked along by the wall, but from her position in the apple tree she could see their hats bobbing up and down.

On entering the garden, the lady waved to Thea and called, "Hello Thea. I can see you hiding in the apple tree."

Thea felt her cheeks burning with embarrassment and shyness which became quite acute as she watched the lady heading in the direction of the apple tree, followed a short distance behind by the man. She rubbed her fingers along the rough lichen-covered branch and wondered what to say.

The lady stood under the tree, smiling, with her arms held out. "Come on, jump," she said. "I want you to come and meet Uncle Robert." From her position on the branch Thea was just a little higher than the lady's hat, which was a mid-blue colour with flowers round the brim. The lady had dark hair, which framed her pale face, and soft brown eyes. Her smile was directed at Thea and her arms were held out to receive Thea's body.

"Come on, darling, come and give Aunty Mary a kiss," she said, "and let me introduce you to Uncle Robert."

Thea slid from the branch, supported by Aunty Mary's out-stretched arms, and landed in the dried grasses at the foot of the apple tree. The lady's eyes and voice were familiar to Thea, but she had no remembrance of her being called Aunty Mary, but felt a great happiness well up inside her when the lady with the pretty blue hat bent down, kissed her warmly on the cheek and covered her with the delicate scent of lavender.

Mammy came to the door smiling, and Mary called out, "Good afternoon, Mrs Clements. We will be with you in a few minutes. We just want to walk round the garden and look at your plants."

"Whenever you are ready," called back Mammy. "I'll have the kettle boiling for tea."

Thea was introduced to Uncle Robert, who was a tall, thin man with blue, slightly bulbous eyes. His hair on the temples was beginning to grey and his Adam's apple protruded at his collar line. He didn't kiss Thea but just patted her on the head.

The breeze made the air cool but there was a golden mellowness to the sun which burnished the autumn flowers with a lacquered brilliance. The decaying odour of the chrysanthemums suggested a hint of frost, and dried leaves rustled the sun's 'swan song'. Several bees, frantically shaking the last sweetness from the year, droned in the bank of Michaelmas daisies.

Robert stood, with his hands behind his back, taking in the cottage and the garden in his gaze. "This is a pretty place, Mary," he said. "Delightful setting and, if the house was done up, it would be a picture."

The house had been an Elizabethan farmhouse, but over the years it had been so heavily used and infrequently repaired that it had lost its gentility and so appeared as a large disorderly cottage. However, it had retained its pleasant proportions, and its timber framing, weathered bricks and thatched roof gave it a kindly appearance. There were six windows at the front which had small leaded panes, three dormer windows that peeped out from under the eyebrows of the thatch and two doors, one going into the sitting room and one into the dairy.

Thea held Aunty's hand and they walked along the stone pathway between the flowers. "The cat had four kittens," blurted out Thea, "but Mammy drowned three."

"Oh dear," replied Aunty Mary sadly, "poor mother cat. She has one kitten, though, and I expect that is as many as she can manage."

When Aunty Mary spoke, the sound triggered a deep-rooted memory in Thea's mind which made her enquire, "Did you take me to the seaside?"

"Fancy you remembering!" exclaimed Aunty Mary. "It was a long time ago. We went with your mother and Aunty Margaret. I've seen you lots of times since then, haven't I? I'm glad that you haven't forgotten going to the seaside. Tell me what you remember."

"We just went, that's all," said Thea quickly, as the images triggered by her aunt's voice hadn't materialized clearly. She watched Vincent swinging from a stout piece of rope fixed to one of the trees in the orchard. "Look at Vince," she said. "Isn't he swinging up high?"

"He will hurt himself if he gets too reckless," replied Aunty Mary. She turned to look for Robert, who was bent down among the plants, examining them in great detail. "Uncle Robert loves plants," she went on. "He would spend all day in the garden."

As they walked near to him he looked up from the plant that he was examining and said, "Has this place got sanitation?"

"Oh no!" replied Mary. "It hasn't got electricity either."

"Hardly suitable for children," murmured Robert.

"I suppose not, really," said Mary, "but countless generations of children have been brought up without either."

"Yes, and plenty have died or been in poor health," retorted Robert. He frowned and walked along the path seeking out more plants.

"We ought to go in," said Mary. "It will appear rude if we stay in the garden."

"I will come in and meet her and then possibly take a walk around," said Robert. "It really is too pleasant a day to be cooped up indoors."

The couple entered the living room of the cottage, with Thea holding tightly to her aunt's hand. Thea watched while everyone shook hands and she was enthralled to hear her aunt say, "I want you to meet my husband, Robert. We came back from honeymoon last evening and we thought before we did anything else we would come and see little Thea."

"Nice to see you, I'm sure," exclaimed Mammy. "Did you have pleasant weather for your honeymoon?"

Thea wondered what a honeymoon was. It was such a funny word.

Mary took off her coat and Tom, rubbing his hands on his trousers, took it from her and hung it on the back of the door. She was wearing a dress exactly the same colour as her hat, with dainty navy-blue shoes which toned beautifully. She sat down in one of the grandfather chairs and lifted Thea on to her lap. Robert sat on the sofa, placing his hat on his knee, while Monica, who had been playing on the floor with some crayons, climbed up and sat beside him, although continuing to crayon.

Thea felt important as she sat cradled in her aunt's arms. She didn't move or say a word, but listened to the conversation that flowed between the adults. Tom and Uncle Robert talked about apples and the best way to stop maggots getting into the fruit, while Aunty Mary and Mammy talked about making pickle.

After a little while Thea suddenly said, "We went to the seaside on the train."

Aunty Mary sounded surprised but delighted and said, "Do you know this child has a marvellous memory for she was only two when we went to Cornwall. I'm amazed she remembers anything, because she was quite miserable all through the holiday. It was all too much for her, too strange, that is why we haven't taken her since."

"Did you take her on holiday then?" enquired Mammy.

"Yes, Mabel, Margaret and myself took her to the cottage in Cornwall," said Mary.

Thea remembered how frightened she had been when the three strange ladies had taken her on the train. She had seen trains since; in fact many times a day they rushed along the track by the school and she knew they were nothing to fear, but at her first meeting with the monster it had hissed, snorted, rumbled and moved its wheels in the most menacing manner.

She realised now that it was Mabel who picked her up to look at the engine, just as a column of shrieking steam had been ejected. She screamed and Mabel had been very annoyed, so annoyed that she had opened the carriage door and pushed her in heavily on to a seat.

"Is she never going to stop yelling and crying," Mabel had said in desperation. "Whatever I show her she cries at. You would think she would be interested in a train."

Mabel had sat on the seat opposite and glared out of the window, and it was Mary that had picked up the sobbing Thea to comfort her.

"Children hate change, they like to know where they are," said Mammy. "They only feel secure with the things they know—well, at least when they are little."

Thea sat up on Mary's lap. "I remember the hen," she said excitedly. "I remember the black hen. You said 'Higgledy piggledy, my black hen, she lays eggs for gentlemen'!" Thea had been walking with Aunty Mary along a lane by the side of the sands and a black hen had come out from under a hedge and that was what Aunty Mary had said.

"You were very funny," said Mary, "and you kept wanting me to say it again and again." She laughed and cuddled Thea closely to her.

Thea knew that the other grown-ups were impatient and wanted to move on along the beach, but she had wanted to stay with Aunty Mary and the black hen for ever.

"Uncle Robert and I would like you to spend Christmas with us, Thea," said Mary. "Would you like that?"

Thea said, "Yes," but she was unsure of what Christmas meant; all she knew was that she liked being with Aunty Mary.

"Will her mother be with you?" enquired Mammy. "Or your other sister?"

"Doubtful," answered Mary. "Mabel will be with her friends," she shot a knowing glance at Robert, "and Margaret will possibly be spending Christmas in the south of France."

"Lucky for some. Would you like tea?" Mammy enquired, looking quite disgruntled that anyone should spend Christmas in the south of France.

"We shall have dinner with my parents," went on Mary, "and my younger brother and his latest girlfriend will possibly be there—so it should be fun."

"There are no other children," said Robert, "but that shouldn't worry Thea too much as I am sure she will enjoy the change."

Mammy just grunted and poured the water into the teapot, giving the impression that she didn't have much time for Christmas.

Tea was drunk and the afternoon passed quickly and pleasantly. Marjory and Laurence arrived back breathless from a long bicycle ride. Vincent, tired of swinging in the orchard, decided to stay indoors and make a lot of noise, while Robert and Tom went to the farm to inspect the milking herd, bringing back a strong smell of cowsheds when they returned.

Just as the light was beginning to fade, Robert and Mary caught the bus back to Worcester. Mammy, with Monica and Thea, walked down the lane to see them off. Thea felt a sadness as she saw the bus go and she waved until it disappeared round the bend in the road. In a very short while she forgot about them, because, like all five year old children, she was wrapped up in the present and the urgency of events happening from minute to minute, so it was quite a surprise to her when one day just after school had broken up for the holidays she found that they had arrived at Hacketts Cottage to take her home with them for Christmas.

"We've come, Thea," said Aunty Mary. "Are you all excited?"

Thea was tongue-tied. She wasn't excited, in fact she wasn't anything but confused. She stood in the middle of the living room looking around at Mammy, Tom, Marjory, Vince, Monica and Laurence and didn't want to leave them. The living room and everyone in it were known and secure. She felt that she ought not to leave them, but couldn't say so because she did not want to hurt her Aunty's feelings.

"I've got her case packed," said Mammy. "I think you'll find there is everything she will need."

Thea remained standing in confused silence, unsure of what to say when Laurence broke into her anguish by saying, "I'm going carol-singing tonight."

"I'll come with you," said Thea. "Aunty Mary and Uncle Robert can have tea."

Mary laughed. "No," she said, "we have a car waiting; a friend has driven us across, we mustn't keep him waiting."

Before Thea had a chance to gather her wits, her coat and hat were on and she was in the car with her aunt and uncle driving off along the lanes, leaving the cottage and its inhabitants behind.

Uncle Robert sat by the driver, who was a large man with sandy coloured hair and a florid face. Thea sat with Aunty Mary in the back seat. Fields, woods and telegraph poles whizzed past the window and for a while Thea felt dazed, strange and rather sick. After a time, when she began to relax, she cuddled up closely to Aunty Mary and fell asleep.

It was nearly dark when they arrived at the home of Robert and Mary. Thea woke up suddenly from sleep and shivered as she was lifted out from the car. She stood in the driveway, looking around while her aunt and uncle got the suitcase from the back and chatted to the driver. A large cedar tree held its branches against the pale twilight sky, seeming almost to dwarf the little black and white timbered house.

"Come along," said Mary cheerfully, "let's have tea." She picked up Thea's suitcase and walked towards the door, leaving Robert chatting in the driveway to the sandy-haired man.

On entering the hallway Mary reached for matches and lit a large oil lamp, which had a tall funnel standing in a pale pink bowl. Straight away a tranquil glow filled the small heavily timbered hallway, showing up the polished oak table and the pictures placed along the wall opposite the stairs.

"I'll show you your room in a moment," said Mary, "but first of all let's go into the sitting room and see if the fire is still alight."

The sitting room was a low-ceilinged room dominated by a large open grate. The beams were exposed, as they were in the hallway, and along one wall stood an old Welsh dresser covered in blue and white china. There were three small windows with chintz curtains that matched the chintz covers of the chairs.

Aunty Mary lit two oil lamps, then began to rake the fire. She added some dried sticks to the rather reluctant embers which caused them to burst into flame making the room glow with life. A Christmas tree had been placed in an alcove between two of the windows, draped with tinsel and silver stars.

Thea was enchanted for she had never seen a Christmas tree before, so she felt the feathery tinsel, rubbing it against her cheeks, smelling at the same time the damp woodland smell of the fir.

"After Christmas we shall plant it in the garden," explained Aunty Mary. "We have only taken the tree in, like a guest, to help make our Christmas beautiful."

Thea was delighted with her small bedroom which seemed to be tucked under the eaves. The dormer window looked over the garden and beyond that to the wide sweep of the common. The wallpaper had pink rosebuds on it with a pink counterpane to match. Thea had never slept in a room of her own, so when Aunt Mary kissed her goodnight she felt very lonely and strange in her pretty little room.

The night-light made shadows which jumped and leapt about on the ceiling and walls, making her very afraid. She shut her eyes, pulled the blankets up round her ears and tried to imagine that Monica's small, warm body was beside her in bed.

On Christmas morning Aunty Mary and Uncle Robert called

Thea to their bed. "Come and see what Father Christmas has brought," they called.

Thea got out of bed and tiptoed sleepily to their room, snuggling down between them.

Aunty Mary said, "Look, he has filled your stocking full of presents."

Thea couldn't believe her eyes as Aunty Mary lifted up a bulging black woollen stocking. "Has he left these things for me?" she enquired, hardly believing such a thing could be true.

"Indeed he has," chuckled Robert, with unexpected glee. "It says on the label 'To Thea, because she is a good girl'."

Thea undid package after package. There were pencils, painting books, a pencil case, balloons, sweets and at the bottom, an orange, some nuts and a shining new penny. "I am lucky," she exclaimed. "How did he know where I was staying?"

"Oh, it's all magic," said Mary. "Christmas is all magic. We must get dressed soon because we are going to early service at the church."

Thea put her treasured possessions in a pile on her bed, and looked out of the window. She decided it must be the middle of the night as it was quite dark. Fancy having presents and going to church in the middle of the night. Christmas was indeed strange and magical.

The sky looked like black velvet sprinkled with diamonds and the thistle-down light of the moon showed up the sparkles of frost on the plants and pathway. Thea was enchanted for she couldn't remember seeing stars before, so she stood on the pathway looking up at the sky in wonderment.

"That's the 'Christmas Star'," said Aunty Mary. "It always shines particularly brightly at Christmas time."

To Thea, the air was charged with magic and even the gentle movement of the cedar tree in the frosty wind seemed to be murmuring the Christmas story. Never before had she been aware of such beauty and wonder, which made her reluctant to speak in case everything should vanish away. She held tightly to her aunt's hand, and her aunt held the arm of Robert while the three of them walked quietly along the avenue of lime trees to the church.

The lights shining through the stained-glass windows of the

church showed up the gravestones and the trimmed yew trees. A robin sang from a point above the lychgate, its song striking the thin air with a crystal clarity. Shadows suddenly became people, as they moved towards the lighted porch, and "Happy Christmas. Happy Christmas," floated from the lips of the people.

Once inside the church Thea's senses were overwhelmed with the sound of the organ music, the lights from a hundred candles and the sweet overpowering smell of incense. She looked at the windows with their dazzling colours and the murals on the walls and decided that this church must be where God lived, for she couldn't imagine anywhere more beautiful.

Thea sat between Robert and Mary but with such awe that she felt transported to another world. The music surged, rose and enveloped her in a volume of sound which because of its intensity seemed like a jewelled silence. She looked around in wonder as the choir in white and scarlet vestments drifted down the aisle.

The large golden cross shone reflecting the lamps and candles while the silver incense containers gleamed as they were shaken, exuding a perfumed mist over the people. As the choir floated past they were followed by a tall man dressed in beautiful robes whom Thea supposed must be God.

For the first time in her life she was aware of a unique mystery and sense of occasion, which made her feel like a bird flying in a sunlit sky. In amazement she watched the worshippers, following intently with her eyes their movements and responses, wondering how on earth they could remember what to say or do.

When the service was over, Aunty Mary took her to see the Christmas crib explaining to her who the figures were grouped in the straw. She had been taught something of the story at school, but gazing at the lighted crib in the wonder of the church brought a reality to the story. The tall man in the coloured vestments, who Thea thought must be God, came and spoke to them, so she realized he wasn't God after all, but Canon of the church and a great friend of her aunt and uncle.

The sky was streaked with pink and the moon hung like a pale lantern in the west as they walked out of the church. The bare branches of the lime trees seemed ironed against the sky in which the morning star twinkled brightly. Their footsteps left bruised marks on the frost-encrusted grass and their breath hung heavy and white in the sharp morning air.

Thea thought breakfast would be lovely by the cosy fire, for she suddenly felt very hungry. Aunty Mary had promised a surprise after breakfast and she was filled with a joyful anticipation. Suddenly life was full of unexpected pleasures. She believed Marjory would have liked the church, and she hoped that they were happy at Hacketts Cottage.

The surprise after breakfast was a doll's crib draped in blue and white material. A baby doll dressed in white woollen clothes lay in the crib. Thea was speechless with delight and couldn't believe it belonged to her.

Aunty Mary told her that they were going to have Christmas dinner with Granny and Grandad who lived about a mile away.

"You have never met Granny," said Aunty Mary. "I know she is looking forward to seeing you. Grandad goes to sleep a lot, but I am sure you will like him. Colin, my brother, will be there too, so I know it is going to be fun."

Weak rays of intermittent sunshine fell from a rather heavy sky as Thea, with her aunt and uncle, walked over the common and down the lane to Granny's house. They carried presents in a basket and cradled in Robert's arms was a large potted plant. From some of the windows Christmas trees could be seen winking and paper chains were visible draped from corner to corner of the living room ceilings. It was impossible to see into some of the rooms as a frenzy of steam from the boiling puddings had clouded the windows.

Granny's house was red brick covered in a dark tracery of twisted stems of wisteria. Winter jasmine glinted its acid-yellow petals over the brick porchway and in a sheltered corner between the porch and the wall of the house creamy white porcelain-like Christmas roses looked upwards into the thin air.

Granny, looking through the window, had seen them walking along the garden path, so she had already opened the front door in greeting when they arrived at the porch. She was a small, frail-looking lady in her early sixties, with soft white hair drawn back from her face into a bun. Her delicate complexion had a tissue paper quality to it and her grey eyes were sensitive and sad.

"So this is little Thea," she said softly as she bent down and gathered the child to her. Thea felt the silk of the dress against her face, the musky fragrance and the smallness of the older lady's body. With coat and hat removed, Thea was guided into a spacious sitting room with a cosy fire, and was introduced to an elderly gentleman who was sitting in a large chair by the fire.

"This is Thea, she is staying with us for Christmas," said Mary, pushing Thea towards the elderly gentleman with the flowing hair and white moustache.

"Hello my dear." He bent towards Thea brushing her face with his bristles. "Where do you live?"

"With Mammy and Tom and the others at Hacketts Cottage," replied Thea, stepping back from him and the strong smell that came from the glass that he held in his hand.

"She is staying with us for five days," said Mary cheerily, rubbing her hands against the fire, "but I think it would be nice if she called you Grandad, don't you?"

"Whatever you like, I don't mind what I'm called," he replied, taking a sip from his glass.

A grey uneasiness passed through Thea's mind, a feeling of twilight in the brightness of the day. She suddenly felt a stranger, one who didn't belong. Aunty Mary had talked about Granny and Grandad, but she hadn't introduced Thea to the elderly gentleman as his granddaughter.

"Come with me to the kitchen for a few moments, Mary," said Granny brightly. "Would you like to come too, Thea?" She held her hand towards the child.

As Thea walked out of the room into the hall, she heard Robert say, "Nice little girl. Fostered with some people who live the other side of Worcester." There was a certain tone in Robert's voice that Thea couldn't quite understand, but she had heard the word foster before, and although she couldn't comprehend the expression, she felt in some way different.

Granny opened the oven door and a hot current of air blew across Thea's face. A delicious smell of roast goose filled the kitchen and the fat jumped madly around in the pan. Granny, satisfied with the contents of the oven, busied herself by adjusting lids on the boiling saucepans and putting more water into the saucepan containing the pudding.

Thea sat on the table and looked around Granny's kitchen. She wasn't listening to the conversation of the adults but busied herself looking at the kitchen. It was a large, light room with a window that looked over the garden. The fire in the range gave it a compelling warm feeling. A large Welsh dresser containing pewter plates and mugs ran along one wall, and in the middle of the dresser was a bowl of Christmas roses. A copper warming pan hung on one wall, and there were copper pots arranged on the shelf over the range. In a wicker chair by the side of the range was a large fluffy tabby cat.

She jumped down from the table and sat on the floor by the side of the wicker chair. She ran her fingers through the long silky fur and an amber and black eye opened with suspicion.

"Be careful, dear," warned Granny. "Stroke her gently, as Tabitha is inclined to be spiteful. She is getting rather disagreeable in her old age."

Thea put her lips against the down-like fur of the cat's ear and whispered, "You aren't disagreeable, you are a beautiful Tabitha."

An ominous rumble of warning came from the tabby throat, so Thea ceased stroking, but remained close to the cat, continuing to talk to it gently, getting enormous pleasure from its nearness.

Grandad was in great spirits over dinner. He carved the goose with the skill of a veteran, his thick white hair flopping over his eyes with the effort. He cracked jokes, tickled Thea and made jolly asides to Uncle Robert. After dinner he flopped into his chair by the sitting room fire, undid his waistcoat and promptly went to sleep. He made soft moist sounds through his lips, and his moustache vibrated slightly.

The sitting room was warm and hung with the honeyed smell of Christmas. The fire crackled, Grandad slept, and everyone else talked happily.

Chapter Three

THE small room where Thea lay was situated at the back of the house, overlooking the stack yard of the farm. An aggressive wind blew, which shook the old timbers of the house and shrieked down any lonely crevice it could find. The somewhat senile window frame gave frequent lurches allowing in currents of icy air, enough to move the fragile curtains, while a sleety rain threw itself against the glass making globules of icy water slip downwards in slow procession.

From where she lay in bed, racked with bronchitis, she could see the top of an apple tree, its branches moving wildly like drowning arms in a grey endless sea, seeming more part of the clouds than an expression of the earth's substance.

With a child's exaggerated imagination, she worked out patterns and stories in her mind from the formation of the raindrops, the wild turbulence of the clouds and the movement of the twisted branches. With her eyes just above the blanket, she urged raindrops to race each other as if they were mane-flying horses, seeing within the shapes of the clouds exotic palaces, gallant knights and golden-haired princesses.

For a week she lay feverishly ill in Marjory's room, needing to be on her own because of her restlessness and incessant coughing. Marjory had uncomplainingly given up her room and had slept with Monica. However, when Thea called out at night in her semi-delirious state, it was Marjory who slipped quietly from her bed to attend to her. She would hold the thin, coughing child to her breast to comfort her and give her sips of water or rub camphorated oil into her back to ease her congestion. Mammy tired from her heavy day rarely heard anything. Her body, huge and exhausted, would be sunk into the feather mattress, with the thin, snoring Tom beside her, seeming to be several inches higher than her in the bed.

Marjory's room was small, with one wall panelled in varnished mid-brown wood, a stained wooden floor and a window over-looking the stack yard. Apart from the bed there was only a mahogany chest of drawers in the room and an old wooden chair.

Over the chest of drawers hung two pictures, one of children in Victorian dress snowballing, the other a cross stitch picture with the words *Tell the Truth and Shame the Devil* carefully worked in green and red embroidery cotton. Thea was a little afraid of the pictures, for in her feverish state she felt that the snowballing children were real and would appear from behind the frame becoming part of the room, and the other picture containing the word *Devil* was truly awful.

In the few months that she had been at school she had learnt that 'The Devil' was always lurking about, ready to spring on any unsuspecting wrong-doer. She had seen a picture of him in an old book that was kept in the best parlour. He had horns, hooves, a long tail, a wicked face and a three-pronged fork in his hand. He stuck his fork into anyone who stole or told lies or told tales or walked in woods where trespassers were not allowed.

God, on the other hand, struck people dead for doing the same awful things. It was a question of who got in first with the pun-ishment, but whichever it was there wasn't much to choose between them in Thea's mind. In fact some days life became as difficult as walking through a minefield, so aware was she of wrongs that her nervous system was taut with apprehension.

Other times she forgot about God or the Devil for weeks at a time, until her memory was jolted with the sharp guilty pangs of a lie just told. Then she would wait, with awful dread, for divine retribution to fall. Earthly retribution in the form of slaps and shouts was a pleasant relief, when Thea supposed that God was listening to someone else's lies or the Devil sticking his fork into someone else's backside when the lie was told but she had again luckily escaped.

A cold, wet spell, with a biting north-east wind, had set in after Christmas when Thea returned from her visit to her family. Many days, she and the other children had been soaked through by the time they had arrived at school.

Miss Thomas, sensitive and concerned as ever, had tried frantic-ally to dry their wet coats and shoes. She would stoke up the stove in the classroom and arrange the coats around the fire-guard, placing the shoes belonging to the non-wellington wearers inside the guard to get the extra heat.

The drying garments would steam up the classroom windows, make the room reek of wet sheep and prevent the warmth getting to the children. The problem to the flurried Miss Thomas became a daily headache for she worried desperately about their health.

She brought into school a large iron saucepan so that she could warm their milk over the stove to make them hot cocoa at dinner time. She was convinced that drinking their halfpenny-a-bottle cold milk would do them little good, but that the hot cocoa would ward off chills.

However, in spite of Miss Thomas's efforts, Thea fell victim to the chills. For several days she clung to Joan's hand and had been dragged along the cold, wet lanes, head thumping, legs like jelly, chest rasping, to the school. The effort of the walk left her so exhausted that she had little energy left for books, painting, Miss Thomas's stories, or the kindly prepared hot drink.

After three days of watching the child get progressively more ill, Miss Thomas felt that she must take the position in hand. She asked the vicar, who visited the school every day for morning prayers, if he would kindly give her a lift in his car to Hacketts Cottage, so that she could take Thea home and see that she was put to bed. The vicar graciously agreed to help and so it was that Thea was taken home.

When Mammy opened the cottage door she looked less than pleased to see the school-teacher there and the look on her face suggested that Miss Thomas was interfering and overstepping the boundaries that were of no concern to her.

"The little girl is not well, Mrs Clements. I feel she has a fever," said Miss Thomas with a certain degree of timidity. "I think she would be better off in bed than in the classroom."

Mammy wiped her hands on her apron and gave a slight sniff of disapproval. "It's only a cold," she said, "but she does seem to have a weak chest. She won't eat properly and with this cold wind it doesn't give her chest a chance." She pushed her hair back from her face and looked at Miss Thomas rather fiercely through her steel-framed glasses. "Anyhow, thank you for your bother."

Miss Thomas moved away nervously from the door but before stepping along the path she said, "When Thea is better, I will bring her some reading books, as she does love reading."

"I want her back at school when she is better," retorted Mammy and firmly closed the door.

Shivering violently, Thea undressed, then sank gratefully into Marjory's bed. Mammy made her drink blackcurrant tea and had rubbed her chest with camphorated oil, her big rough hands seeming to tear at the flesh of the sensitive, sore little body. Days of wild delirium then passed, with hours merging into each other, interspersed with bouts of coughing which became a choking nightmare, leaving her sweating, weak and gasping for breath.

She felt that she had been in Marjory's bed always, and the small room was her entire world. Because she felt weak she was content to lie snuggled under the bed–clothes, for whenever she put her arms out of the bed they soon became chilled through the coldness of the room and if she sat up her head began to swim making her feel sick.

After several weeks the chest began to clear and the black rings began to disappear from under her eyes. Slowly she began to gain in strength and the desire to get dressed and to look at books again returned. Vince brought books from school, with kindly messages from Miss Thomas, who, although she would have liked to, thought it better not to visit Hacketts Cottage. Thea greeted the books like old friends and excitedly read about the activities of Rover and Kitty and their long–suffering family.

Once strong enough to walk the lanes, she returned to school, but her attendance was poor throughout the winter as she was often too tired to make the journey. When the east wind blew with its icy knife her chest became congested again and on frosty mornings the sharpness of the air would make her cough uncontrollably. However, when the days became milder, her health gradually improved with a pink glow returning to her cheeks.

She loved school and would much rather be there than at home. The smell of chalk dust, old books, combined with the strong sulphurous smell of the stove, created a haven for her. Miss Thomas's quiet authority was a constant comfort and reassurance to her, however turbulent the morning might have been. The teacher patiently showed the children a new and sparkling world through her eyes. She pointed out the wild flowers, the birds and the changing seasons, creating for the children a world of wondrous fascination.

Bright colours were mixed in pots, and infants, who had never before held a paint brush in their hands, experienced the exuberant satisfaction of blending rainbows together on sheets of blank paper, with the occasional slip of the brush which streaked other's faces. Songs were sung, poems read, games played and reading books devoured like fondants, making the days pass by in a kaleidoscopic medley of images and impressions. Rarely was a sharp word spoken or a tear shed, so harmonious was the atmosphere of the little village schoolroom.

During the Easter holidays, Mabel turned up unexpectedly—as far as Thea was concerned—and announced that she was going to take her shopping. Thea couldn't remember when she had last seen Mabel, so it was quite a surprise to see her standing there, sparkling, self-assured and bent on a shopping expedition.

"What are you going to buy?" asked Mammy, somewhat disconcerted.

"A whole new outfit for Thea," retorted Mabel. "All her clothes are shabby and she needs smartening up." She looked at Thea with a critical eye and said suddenly, "She's got thinner, she looks awful."

"She has been ill, you know she has," said Mammy defensively. "I told you how ill she had been—had weeks off school and lost a lot of weight."

Mabel cast a guilty glance in the direction of her daughter and said, "Her hair looks all scraggy and dull. Hasn't it been washed?"

Mammy, greatly put out by the remark, said, "Of course it has been washed, but hair is always lifeless if a person is unwell." Folding her arms across her ample bosom, she seemed to rise several inches in height before saying, "I feel you should have visited the child, especially during her illness. It's too bad to put all the responsibility on to me."

Mabel flushed and looked embarrassed, but said that she had been unable to get away because of the pressure of work.

Mammy sniffed in a disbelieving manner and said that she believed children should always come first; it had always been her policy to put the children first, but some people had different ideas.

For a moment it seemed that the atmosphere was about to explode but the situation was saved by the entrance of Laurie who, seeing Mammy's grim set face, went up to her, put his arm round her shoulder and hugged her. The old lady immediately relaxed and bitter argument was prevented.

Mammy was very attached to Laurence, having brought him up from a fortnight old. His mother, a thin, frightened girl, had taken him to Hacketts Cottage to be cared for until she could get her accommodation sorted out. That was the last time Mammy or anyone else had seen her. She had left no name or address, only her fragile possession who had grown up into a strong, healthy and attractive boy. At the grammar school he was at the top of his year and his masters predicted a fine future for him. Mammy often reflected on how she would cope if his natural mother ever return- ed, but as the years passed by the chances of it happening had become more remote.

Mabel, trying to overcome the ill–feeling she had engendered, suggested that Mammy might like to go shopping with her, but her offer was refused under the pretext of pressing duties that must be carried out that afternoon. Mabel combed Thea's hair, washed her face, buttoned her into a black school coat and took her into Worcester shopping.

Mabel seemed ill at ease sitting on the bus amongst the Saturday shoppers, and Thea sensing the awkwardness of the situation kept her eyes firmly fixed on the window. She could see Mabel's reflec- tion in the glass and noticed how her pretty face was disgruntled and pouting. When they got off the bus Mabel propelled her with impatient haste into the children's section of the department store. There Thea stood in her vest and knickers while various dresses were pulled on and off her.

"She's so thin," Mabel complained to the assistant. "Nothing seems to fit her, and her hair—look at it."

She stood miserably by allowing clothes to be put on and taken off. Her shoulders were thumped, her chest tapped, her back smoothed, and eventually Mabel was satisfied and a selection of dresses, socks and under–clothes were parcelled up and put into a large bag. Her opinion had not been asked and she was given no opportunity to say whether she liked or disliked any of the gar- ments that had been unceremoniously tried on her.

"Now," said Mabel, "We'll do something about that hair, and see if we can't make you look a bit more human."

Thea followed meekly behind Mabel who was trotting as briskly as her high heels would allow. She carried her large parcel in front of her in both arms, and her pretty chestnut brown hair bobbed up and down as she moved. She turned into a hair dressing salon and with relief let go of the package.

"Can you do anything with this girl's hair," she asked a blonde, elegant stylist.

Thea feeling like the package that Mabel had just deposited on the salon chair, shuffled uneasily as the stylist picked up pieces of her hair and sniffed disapprovingly at it.

"Do you want it bobbed and washed?" she asked.

"Anything that will make it look better," said Mabel.

"What do you usually wash it in? It's very dry and lifeless."

Mabel appearing to look surprised said, "She doesn't live with me —I'm just taking her out."

The stylist placed a board across the chair and sat Thea on it. She looked at herself in the large mirror and could see Mabel also looking. She was patting her hair and smoothing her eye brows and then when she saw the child looking she turned away as if self conscious.

"Cut a fringe," she said, "and shape it so that her ear lobes just show. I think a change of style might alter her appearance."

The stylist nodded approvingly, and began to chop away at the straggly brown locks, while Mabel moved away and settled herself in the corner with a magazine.

When they had finished at the salon, Mabel walked with the child along the river bank. She had ordered a taxi to take them back to Hacketts Cottage, for she couldn't face struggling on the bus with her parcel. There was half an hour to spare before it was due, which didn't allow enough time to have tea, so Mabel decided that a walk would be the best thing.

"Are you pleased with your new clothes?" she asked.

"Yes," replied Thea politely, feeling more puzzled than pleased. She couldn't imagine when she would wear the green silk dress with the white collar, or the straw hat with the ribbons hanging down the back. In fact the hat had already loomed as a great burden, for she was certain it would fall off and get trodden on.

"I'm going to take you to see your godmother in two weeks time," explained Mabel, "and I want you to look as nice as possible."

Thea nodded her head wondering what on earth a godmother

could be. She reasoned that she must be the sister of a grandmother.

"I shall want you to be very good and polite, and to be on your best behaviour. I shan't expect you to let me down."

"I won't," replied Thea in a small fearful voice, but she had no idea what she was supposed to do to please Mabel. She looked at the river sparkling in the spring sunlight, and the acid yellow forsythia splashed against the mellow stones of the Bishop's Palace.

"Are you happy with Mrs Clements?"

The question was so direct and unexpected that it startled Thea. "I'm happy," she said, having no yardstick to measure happiness by.

"Does she hit you?"

Thea was just about to say 'sometimes when I'm naughty', but a sudden feeling of loyalty overcame her, and she said, "No."

"Never!" exclaimed Mabel in disbelief.

Thea thought of the hard slaps she had received, and the punishment of being shut in the cold, dark cupboard without any clothes on, but she persisted in saying, "No," for she felt safer with Mammy than she did with Mabel.

Mabel greeted a vacant riverside seat with a whoop of relief, sitting down thankfully with her parcel beside her. She was silent for a few moments, then she asked, "Did you enjoy Christmas with Aunty Mary?"

Thea started with surprise, for Christmas seemed so long ago that she had almost forgotten. She looked at Mabel awkwardly and nodded her head.

"Do you like Aunty Mary and Uncle Robert?" Mabel persisted.

Thea nodded again, and Mabel sighed, for she found it a burden trying to communicate with the child.

One morning, two weeks later, Mammy packed Thea's best clothes, explaining to her that she was going away for the weekend with Mabel. Mammy was going to take her into Worcester where Mabel would meet them.

Sitting on the bus rattling along the green lanes, Thea felt as prim and exotic as a potted plant, dressed in her new silk dress and straw hat with ribbons hanging down the back. She was almost afraid to move in case the hat fell off, or the dress became creased.

At an appointed place, Mabel was sitting in a chauffeur-driven car. Looking cool and elegant in a cream suit with navy-blue edgings, she waved at them through the open window. Thea got into the car by the side of her, and Mammy, a heavy shabby figure with a tired lined face, waved them goodbye.

The car purred along the lanes while Thea and Mabel sat back in the luxuriant upholstery and gazed, each through their own window. They said little to each other; the only comments made were those that Mabel uttered expressing delight at a brilliant field of buttercups or an extraordinarily attractive cottage garden. Thea felt uneasy. She didn't know what to say. She sensed, with a childlike awareness, that their relationship was not normal, and that she was the cause of some embarrassment to the older woman.

At a bend in the lane, a range of silvery hills appeared, suddenly and unexpectedly, rising out of the chequered fields. The range lay across the plain like a huge sleeping dinosaur with clouds on its back. With delight she saw that the shape of the hills was familiar; they were the same hills that were visible from Aunty Mary's house. Her heart felt lighter as the car climbed upward into the hilly greenness, and eventually entered a gate which went off a steep road sweeping into a long driveway between an avenue of trees.

The house was set back under the lee of the hill, being completely hidden from the road by a wood of mixed deciduous trees, interspersed with cedars and Norwegian spruce. It was a substantially built house of natural stone, with heavy gables and square bay windows. A large conservatory had been built against one of the wings of the house, and through its open doors white wicker chairs could be seen with a profusion of plants pressing against the glass.

Scattered about in front of the house were various articles belonging to its young occupants, such as a toy truck, a hoop, a bicycle and a pony tethered to a lilac tree, who looked towards the car with sharp-eyed interest. A large Red Setter dog chased excitedly into the driveway from the back of the house as they got out of the car.

The chauffeur, shouting to the dog to stop its noise, took the suitcase, ran up the steps and rang the front door bell.

Much to Thea's surprise, Mabel suddenly said to her, "Don't tell any of our secrets. It's best to keep some things to ourselves, so be careful what you say."

She couldn't imagine for one moment what Mabel meant because as far as she knew, she hadn't got any secrets. Perhaps Mabel wanted her to keep quiet about the new dresses, and not to mention the price of the shoes.

A middle-aged lady in a neat dark dress answered the door, she greeted them pleasantly, and told them that everyone was in the garden but she had been requested to take them through.

"Everyone is making the most of the sunshine," she said. "The lawn at the back of the house is such a suntrap, until the sun goes behind the hill."

The large hall was cool with its marble tiled floor, but seemed almost gloomy after the brightness of the outside. The Red Setter pushed in front of them to lead them into the garden, his feet making soft sounds on the stone. White lilac in a copper container standing on a dark chest threw out a heavy fragrance. At the end of the hallway was a door which led into the garden.

Thea looked with amazement into the garden. There were so many people, but no one she knew. A plump older lady in a mauve dress came towards them with outstretched hands. "My darlings, so lovely to see you." She brushed Mabel's cheek and patted Thea's head. "You've grown Thea," she exclaimed.

Thea was surprised, for she couldn't remember seeing the lady before. "Is she my godmother?" she whispered to Mabel.

"Of course she's your godmother, I told you I was bringing you to see her," replied Mabel dismissively, separating herself from the small damp hand.

Thea stood rooted to the spot watching children and dogs tearing around the garden. Mabel was chatting to a group of ladies in summery frocks, apparently unaware that Thea hadn't immediately flung herself headlong into play with the other children.

A saving hand was suddenly placed on her shoulder. "I'm Nanny Davis," said a soft voice, "Come and meet Isabelle and Gloria."

Thea turned and looked into the gentle smiling face of a lady wearing a starched white cap and apron. "Isabelle, Gloria," she called. "Come and meet your visitor."

Two fair-haired girls jumped off the swing under the cedar tree and ran boisterously across the lawn. "Who is it?" The older girl called, "Who is our visitor?"

"Don't shriek so," cautioned Nanny Davis, "It's so rude. This is Dorothea who has come to spend the night with you."

Shocked at the strangeness of the name Dorothea, Thea said boldly, "I'm called Thea."

"All right, Thea," laughed Nanny Davis, "I'm sorry I got the name wrong. This is Isabelle and Gloria."

For a few moments the girls gazed at each other uncertainly, then Gloria, the younger of the girls, said, "Are you our cousin?"

Thea, uncertain of what a cousin was, said, "The lady over there is my godmother."

"Oh," chuckled Isabelle, "that's our grandmother—what do you call her?"

Thea shrugged her shoulders, for she had no idea what she was supposed to call her. Mabel had just said you are going to meet your godmother, but she didn't give her a name.

"Well off you go and play together," chirped Nanny Davis, "and don't push Thea too high, she may not be used to it."

"Do you say your prayers to our grandma?" said Gloria, grabbing Thea's hand and racing with her across the lawn.

"No," gasped Thea, "I don't say prayers to her. Am I supposed to?"

Peels of silvery laughter exploded from Isabelle. "Silly thing Gloria, of course she doesn't have to keep saying prayers. God-mothers just give you presents."

Thea running along with the girls towards the swing, couldn't see the connection between prayers and presents, and the concept of the word godmother became even more puzzling, particularly when she looked like an ordinary lady and was also other children's grandmother—and she certainly didn't give her presents.

Gloria jumped on one of the swings and began to work her legs so that the swing went higher and higher, her fair hair cascading out behind her. Isabelle helped Thea on to the other swing and gently pushed her.

"Who are all the other children?" asked Thea tentatively, "and all the ladies?"

"Aunts and cousins," replied Isabelle matter of factly. "No uncles this weekend, just boring old aunts and horrible boy cousins."

Thea noticed two older girls sitting apart from the vigorous hide and seek going on in the shrubbery. "Who are they?" she enquired.

"Oh, they are Angela and Stella." There was a disparaging tone to Isabelle's voice. "They never play with us, they think they are too grown up." She gave Thea a harder push, "They are our cousins, our oldest cousins."

Thea, taking her courage in both hands, asked, "What is a cousin?"

"The children of your parents' brothers or sisters, they are your cousins. Don't you know that?"

"I haven't got any," gasped Thea, trying to accustom herself to the force of the swing.

"You haven't got any cousins?" Isabelle's voice rang with incredulity.

Thea, ashamed of such a deficit, shook her head and whispered, "I haven't got cousins." Her head swam with the movement of trees and bushes, her mind jumbled up in a confusion of colours and impressions. The garden echoed to shrieks of laughter, and the dogs chased each other excitedly, barking loudly. When the swing was brought to a standstill, Thea found herself looking into Isabelle's questioning blue eyes.

"Why is my grandmother your godmother?" she asked.

Thea was nonplussed. "I don't know," she replied timidly. "I don't know why there are godmothers." She glanced across the lawn at Nanny Davis retrieving a small boy from the rose-bed. "Why is she wearing a funny hat?" she asked.

"It's not funny, it's what nurses always wear. Doesn't your nurse wear a cap then?"

Thea shook her head, feeling suddenly overwhelmingly inadequate for not possessing a nurse, a cousin or a dog. It was all so new and bewildering, and quite beyond her understanding.

"Come on," called Gloria, "let's play hide-and-seek with the others." And that is what they did, until hot and exhausted they were ushered in to tea.

The children ate apart from the adults, supervised by the nurses. It was a jolly noisy meal, and the boys were particularly exuberant, having got thoroughly wound up by their games before tea. Thea began to feel more relaxed, but she said little, although she was surprised by the rowdy behaviour. At home the children were made to eat quietly round the table, as Mammy got very cross if they didn't.

After tea, all but the youngest children went back out to play, but Isabelle asked Thea if she would like to choose some games from the toy cupboard and play with her indoors. Thea felt she would agree with anything Isabelle suggested, so together they went along to the huge toy cupboard which was on one of the landings.

When Isabelle opened the doors, Thea was astonished by the assortment of toys of all sorts that the cupboard contained. Some of the toys were well-used, having a much-loved air about them, as they had belonged to the children's parents, while others had been newly added to the collection and stood in clean, crisp boxes, inviting inspection.

A group of teddy bears with sad neglected eyes were huddled in a wicker chair, for the small boy who had once loved them was an executive in the city. Thea rearranged them in the chair and kissed their almost furless heads, while Isabelle hunted up and down the shelves for a game that she thought they would both enjoy.

Selecting a box, Isabelle took Thea's hand, led her away from the teddy bears and together they went downstairs.

The drawing room overlooked the garden, and at the open French windows sat Mabel with Thea's godmother. They were talking and seemed relaxed in each other's company and they raised no objections when the little girls entered the room and began to play Chinese chequers on the carpet.

Sounds of the children playing hide-and-seek in the garden drifted into the room, accompanied by the wild barks from the dog, but the frolics didn't encourage Isabelle and Thea to join them, they were happier in the warm intimacy of each other's company than in being with the others.

"I'm glad you have a reliable nurse for the child." Thea heard her godmother say.

To the child's astonishment Mabel replied, "An excellent person; couldn't be better. She is happy living in the country in a place I have. I go when I can. It's a very good arrangement."

Thea paused in her game, looking in the direction of the women, but an expression in Mabel's eyes warned her to be quiet and get on with her game.

"Come on, Thea," said Isabelle, giving a tug at Thea's dress, "your move."

"A very kind person," went on Mabel, "and a first class disciplinarian, but quite devoted to the child."

"I'm with Mammy and Tom," Thea blurted out.

Mabel ignoring her continued, "It isn't easy, but it's the best arrangement we can find."

"Does she have companions of her own age?" asked Thea's godmother.

"Just at the school," replied Mabel.

"There is Monica and Marjory and Vince . . ." stammered Thea.

Mabel got up and taking the child's arm, firmly propelled her out of the room. Looking back she said apologetically, "She needs the lavatory."

Once outside the door, Mabel shook her vigorously and dragged her along the hallway. "I told you to behave yourself," she hissed, "I told you not to let me down."

Thea speechless with amazement choked, "I haven't."

"Yes, you have, talking about Mrs Clements and those children."

"Why can't I talk about them?"

"Because I don't want you to talk about them—do you understand? A nanny looks after you—now you just keep your mouth shut."

She pushed Thea back towards the room. "Now you listen to me, you are not to say anything about where you live or who looks after you. Quite clear?"

"Yes," Thea gasped, but she didn't understand, neither could she fathom why Mabel was so cross.

Mabel, smiling sweetly, opened the door of the drawing room, returning as if nothing had happened.

Thea's throat felt tight and her heart began to bump wildly in her rib cage, she couldn't think why Mabel was telling such lies.

Sensing Thea's disinterest in the game, Isabelle said suddenly, "Shall I get the snakes and ladders, Thea? I'm sure you would like a game of those."

Isabelle picked up the Chinese chequers, and putting them back into the box, walked out of the room. The sun had gone behind the hill, and the room was shaded and quiet. The two women continued to talk by the open window and, apart from their voices and the occasional shouts from the garden, the only sound was the clear notes of a blackbird singing.

Little waves of uneasiness shot through Thea's body, for suddenly the atmosphere felt chill. In her young mind she couldn't understand why Mabel didn't tell her godmother about Mammy and the other children and Tom. Why did she pretend that Mammy was her nurse, and that they lived alone and that Mabel spent every weekend with them? It all seemed quite preposterous, but she had been ordered to be quiet.

"Oh, the school is first-class," Mabel's voice broke into her thoughts. "I am delighted with the school, and she is coming on so well." Thea loved school and she was pleased that Mabel had mentioned her school. Miss Thomas wasn't a lie and she loved Miss Thomas very much.

Isabelle returned and put the game of snakes and ladders on to the floor. She smiled at Thea and said, "I hope you know the rules of snakes and ladders, Thea. Right, you shake the dice first."

Together the little girls sat on the floor and played until Nanny Davis appeared and led them to bed. Thea slept in a bed which was underneath the window in Isabelle's room and Gloria slept in the same room as her nanny. The window was open allowing in the scents and sounds of the late spring evening. Isabelle had fallen almost immediately to sleep, but Thea couldn't sleep, her mind was a mixed confusion of images from the day.

The harsh, vibrating croaking of the nightjar disturbed the otherwise gentle sounds of evening and gave the soft air an eerie overtone. The larch trees sighed like distant waves and the nightingale sang from the woods. It was the first time in her young life that Thea had been totally aware of so much sound.

She lay listening until the black stillness of the night wrapped the countryside up in silence, and the darkness bore down on her and she tossed and turned in her bed. She would have been afraid if it weren't for the thistledown breaths coming from Isabelle's bed.

Just as dawn was beginning to edge into the eastern sky she fell into a heavy sleep and when she awoke she found to her amazement that the room was full of sunlight and Isabelle's bed empty. In panic she jumped from the bed and ran to the window in time to see

Angela and Stella leading their ponies back to the stables in the company of the red dog.

Disconcertedly she scrambled into her clothes and without bothering to comb her hair, ran downstairs in search of her companions. The house seemed so enormous that she didn't know in which direction to aim. Opening the first door at the foot of the stairs, she entered a room smelling of polish, containing a large table and a sideboard covered in silver dishes. Bending over, polishing a chair with tremendous vigour, was a young parlour maid. She looked at Thea with large surprised eyes and said, "Can I help you, Miss?"

"I was looking for Isabelle and Gloria," said Thea. "Do you know where they are?"

"Don't know," replied the maid, "but Madam is eating breakfast in the Morning Room across the hall," she jerked her finger in the direction of the room, "and the younger members I expect are having breakfast in the day nursery."

"Thank you," Thea muttered, as she crossed the hall, opened the door of the morning room, and there she found her godmother, with Isabelle and Gloria's mother, sitting drinking tea.

She was unsure of what to say, but her godmother sensing the situation, stretched out her arms and said, "Hello my sweet, have you just woken up? Come and sit on my lap and have a cup of tea."

Picking Thea up and placing her on her lap, she said, "You're a thin scrap, like a little feather. The children are taking the donkeys up the hills. Would you like to go too?"

"Yes, I would like to go with Isabelle and Gloria," replied Thea, sipping her tea.

"Have you seen Nanny?" enquired the girls' mother, "and have you had breakfast?"

Thea shook her head, but she wasn't greatly interested in break-fast. However, her godmother cut up bacon and egg and, putting her in a chair by the side of her, insisted that she eat before going out on the hills.

She felt greatly privileged as she knew the others would be eating in the nursery and, although she would rather have been with them, she didn't wish to offend her godmother, so she quietly ate it up.

Isabelle and Gloria's mother looked at the child with a mixture of compassion and bewilderment, and then at her mother. "Sometimes I think you are rather strange," she said.

"Why?" the older woman replied.

"Asking them, when we are all here."

"Surely it's the time to ask them when there is company for the child."

"I know, but I think it's peculiar—really I do."

"She works for me, and I've known her for years."

"I know, mother."

"Well she is almost family."

"No she isn't, and you know it."

Thea looked up from her bacon and eggs, sensing that they were talking about her and Mabel. Both women smiled encouragingly at her so she continued to eat.

"Nothing will come of it, they'll stay together."

The older woman made a gesture of hopeless resignation with her hands. "I'm sure you are right my dear, but am I to ignore the little scrap, pretend it doesn't exist?"

"I feel sorry for them both. It's wrong somehow, that people should be so miserable."

She laughed. "No one is miserable my dear. I've learnt to live with situations I cannot alter, make the best of things, that's my motto."

After Thea had eaten, her godmother took her up to the nursery where an air of lively exuberance was prevailing amidst an over-whelming smell of bacon and eggs.

"There you are," shouted Isabelle. "You were asleep when I got dressed. We are taking the donkeys out. You are coming, aren't you?"

"You'll need shorts," said Gloria. "Have you got shorts?"

The older woman smiled tolerantly at the abundance of high spirits amidst the atmosphere of profound chaos, but told one of the nurses to get Thea properly dressed for riding the donkey, and explained to her that the child had eaten breakfast. She kissed the baby and quietly slipped away from the noise to the relative peace of downstairs.

The donkeys were brought round from the sheds by an auburn haired youth, covered in freckles and grinning from ear to ear.

"Which one are going to let your visitor ride, Master Richard?" enquired the youth, straightening out the harness.

"Give her Polly," called Richard. "Polly is fairly dopey, she won't buck."

Thea looked with apprehension at the donkey but she had no intention of letting on that she had never ridden before. "Come on," said the auburn-haired youth, "Jump on, Miss, I'll give you a hand." With a strong arm he lifted Thea up into the saddle and adjusted her sandals to the stirrups. Before Thea had hardly had time to grasp the enormity of her position the donkey began to move, following the disappearing line of donkeys that were quickly heading up the hill path by the side of the house.

The donkey boy ran in front, giving Richard's donkey a slap across the flank which made it run at a fair gallop in spite of the heat and the steep pathway. The other donkeys hurried after and the little train of animals headed for the broad, flat path which curved around the hill.

Nanny Davis suddenly appeared through a gate at the side of the garden and joined the group. Thea heard her voice call, "John, Richard, Paul, now don't get too wild and remember it's hot for the donkeys today." The boys on their donkeys disappeared round the hill path, and Nanny Davis walked briskly behind Isabelle's and Gloria's donkeys, urging them not to go so quickly.

Thea felt very apprehensive on the donkey, but she clung to the reins with tense white knuckles, hoping against hope that she wouldn't suddenly desire to gallop with the others. She looked around her from the very different position of a donkey's back and was amazed at how altered the world appeared. It was like being on stilts peering over the shrubs and bushes. The houses in the patchwork valley seemed too small for human habitation and everything appeared asleep. The land fell in a series of green fields until it was lost in the blue haze of a distant horizon.

Turning the bend in the hill path, Thea noticed, much to her astonishment, that the boys and their donkeys were way up, nearly to the summit of the next hill, and she could just see the top of Isabelle's head in a fold between the hills, with the blue of Nanny Davis's dress walking beside Gloria's donkey. The auburn-haired donkey boy was sitting on the side of the path, some distance ahead, waiting for Thea. He waved his arms and called, "Come on, Miss, you're getting all behind."

Thea had no idea how you made a donkey go quicker or slower, but she was suddenly filled with a choking fear that the boy would run up to her, slap the donkey and make it gallop. She wished the boy would get up and run after Gloria's donkey and leave her alone.

A hundred yards or so from where the youth sat, Thea's donkey suddenly stopped and started to pull at some grass in the bank at the side of the path. Seizing the opportunity, she slipped her feet from the stirrups and slithered down the donkey's flanks on to the path. She held on to the reins, looked at the donkey's face and at the grass protruding from its soft lips. She was aware of how sad the donkey looked, with its downcast eyes, long eyelashes and drooping ears.

Overcome with emotion, she pressed her face against the donkey's mane and said, "It's all right, I won't make you walk up the hill, I will stay here with you and you can eat all the grass you want. Will that make you happy, Polly Donkey?"

The donkey gave a small disinterested shake of the head and pulled another tuft of grass from the bank. She drew her hand across its broad hard forehead down to the soft fleshy part of its nose where the warm air came out in soft snorts from the effort of munching the grass.

"Come on," called the donkey boy. "What are you hanging about for?"

"We aren't coming any further," said Thea. "We are staying here. The donkey wants to eat grass."

"We've got to catch the others up," called the boy. "They will be out of sight in a moment. Get back on the donkey and I'll make her go. Polly is a lazy donkey."

He made to walk towards Thea, but she turned obstinately in his direction and called, "I am not coming. I'm staying here. You go with the others."

Realizing that pleading was no good and not knowing how to cope with the strange little girl, he turned and ran after the distant donkeys calling, "She won't come. She says she is going to stay."

Still holding the reins Thea sat in the grass close to the moving mouth of the donkey. The grass exuded a warm, sweet smell while the sun beat down strongly on her head. She looked with fascination at the uncurling fronds of bracken that were all around, some just forcing their way up through the peaty soil, with others standing triumphant and erect among the brown of last season's bracken.

She stroked one of the heads of bracken and tried to straighten its curled leaves. a brightly coloured peacock butterfly danced with jerky, erratic movements over a May bush nearby, and a green lizard flashed across a warm pink stone, stopping momentarily to blink at its small world, not comprehending the donkey or the girl.

"Why aren't you coming with us?" Nanny Davis's voice floated across the hill and her blue figure was visible running along the path. "Is Polly being difficult?"

Thea looked towards her and was amazed at how small her figure looked against the vastness of the hill and yet how clearly her voice travelled, so it seemed there was little distance between them.

Panting slightly and very pink in the face from the exertion of running back along the path, Nanny Davis arrived at the spot where Thea and the donkey were. "What are you doing, dear?" she said. "Why didn't you follow us?"

"She doesn't want to come," said Thea. "She is tired and she is crying." Tears welled up in her eyes and she looked despairingly at the older woman.

Nanny Davis sat down beside her on the bank, taking hold of her hand. "No, my dear, she is used to walking on the hills; in fact she loves the hills."

"She looks so sad," Thea blurted out. "Her eyes are so sad. She won't look at me and smile."

"Little donkeys do look sad, but that is just how they are made, but they are really very happy inside. I'll tell you what," said Nanny cheerfully, "you get back on the donkey and I'll walk beside you, and we'll stop under the trees there on the next hill and if Polly is unhappy we won't go a step further."

Thea stood up, brushed the pieces of last season's dry bracken from her short legs and wiped her eyes with her grubby fingers, making streaks of dirt down her flushed cheeks.

With a burst of sunshine across her face, she looked at the bank where she had been sitting and said, "Look, I've made quite a nest. Look, Nanny, at the place where I have been sitting."

Nanny Davis smilingly lifted the little girl back on to the donkey and together they set off along the hill path. When they rounded the bend of the hill, they could see Isabelle and Gloria waiting for them in the valley between the hills. The boys were no longer visible but the donkey boy could be seen as a moving dot climbing the distant hill.

Like extravagant icing on a cake, the elder blossom showed flamboyant patches among the gold of the gorse. The sky was high, wide and still and a soft light fell on the little town nestled at the foot of the rounded hills. A thyme scented wind blew across the sorrel which rustled gently in the brown dryness of the previous season's bracken.

Sheep, like pieces of dirty cotton wool, were visible on the distant hills and, near to, they panted in the hot sun, looking up with pale elongated eyes.

"They need their coats off," said Nanny.

Across the hills sounded the bleating of a grown lamb trying to get contact with its mother. Although quite able to cope on its own, its voice was full of plaintive longing.

"What do they do with their coats?" enquired Thea.

"Make them into jumpers and blankets," came the reply.

Thea puzzled at the reply, unable to see the connection. A sheep hunched against a gorse bush was slowly ruminating with rhythmic circular movements of its jaw. She allowed a somewhat apathetic maternal instinct to surface and replied hoarsely to her juvenile.

"Can they take their own coats off?" enquired the child.

"No, silly Billy, the farmer takes them off," said Nanny, waving her arms in the direction of Isabelle and Gloria. They looked like two flaxen-haired dolls flung on the ground but they waved pale arms gaily, and Thea felt a surge of exuberance and joy that they should be pleased to see her.

Chapter Four

THE seat where Mary sat sewing was in deep shadow facing the east side of the house. In the heat of the August afternoon it was the coolest place in the garden, whereas in the early morning it was the sunniest and most sheltered spot. Thea sat on a rug at her aunt's feet struggling with a large needle and a piece of cloth, attempting to sew the edges.

She had been living with her aunt and uncle for just over two months, ever since the weekend that she had spent at her god-mother's house. When the chauffeur had driven away that after-noon, she had unquestioningly thought that the car would be taking them to Worcester and that Mammy would be waiting in the same spot where they had left her, but much to her surprise the car had stopped at Aunty Mary's house.

The last time that Thea had seen her aunt and uncle was at Christmas time, and she was amazed how different everything looked. The black and white thatched cottage seemed dwarfed by all the surrounding abundant greenery that it appeared to spring from the flower beds rather like a fairy story cottage.

Margaret, the younger sister of Mary and Mabel, was there, together with Granny, whom Thea thought looked smaller and frailer than she had remembered. Aunty Margaret was a tall, big-boned, dark-haired lady, who spoke in a direct and authorit-ative manner, seeming very much to influence her sisters.

Thea sat among the grown-ups fascinated by their conversation. It soon became clear that her Grandad had died and that a family conference was being called to see if Granny needed help in any way. She flicked through the pile of books which had been placed at her disposal while listening avidly to the flow of opinions and contra-opinions.

The next morning Mabel got ready to leave and Thea, assuming that she was going too, asked if she should fetch her case.

"You're staying here," said Mabel. "You are going to live with Aunty Mary."

"What, for always?" enquired Thea.

"I don't know about always, but you aren't going back to Mrs Clements."

"Why?" Thea's voice was timid, and a picture of Mammy standing, large and brown, on the pavement waving goodbye flashed into her mind.

"She isn't suitable," said Mabel quickly. "Anyhow, it's the best for you. We have discussed it and we have decided that you should stay here."

Thea felt her cheeks suddenly burn and her heart begin to thump. She felt resentful because no one had included her in the conversation; she had merely been informed of what was to happen.

"Shall I see them again?" she blurted out.

Mabel folded a dress, putting tissue paper carefully between the folds. Thea sat on the window-sill watching. "It depends," said Mabel. "There isn't much to see her about, though."

"I've left lots of things there," said Thea.

"I'll get them sent to you," said Mabel defensively. Turning quickly aside she looked at her daughter and said, "I thought you liked Aunty Mary and Uncle Robert?"

"I do," replied Thea, "but I feel we should explain to Mammy."

"I shall write," said Mabel sharply. "Anyhow, they won't care, you are nothing to them, why should they care? I paid for Mrs Clements to look after you. You were just part of her work, so why should she bother?"

Thea looked through the window, across the common to the line of gentle hills. It was true she loved her aunt, but she thought Mammy liked her too in a sort of way. The idea of being part of someone's job didn't appeal to her.

"Don't you like Mammy?" said Thea. She turned suddenly, looking at Mabel, who was carefully wrapping a pair of high heeled shoes in tissue paper and squeezing them down the side of the suitcase.

"Not particularly," came the reply. "She is a very rough country woman, and not the sort of person that I would choose to bring you up." The suitcase was closed with a final, firm thump and Mabel picked it up and made her way out of the room.

Thea remained on the window-sill wrapped in thought. She felt that Mammy would be upset, as would Monica and Marjory. They would wonder where she was. Miss Thomas would wonder too, especially when the register was being called. She thought of Topsy and Mervyn and kind Joan who took her to school, and tears began to fill her eyes, making the garden swim.

She wondered why she hadn't been told of the decision and it made her feel very unimportant. She rubbed her face against the curtains, watching her tears soak into the fabric.

After a little while Mabel's voice called up the stairs quite cheerfully, "Goodbye, Thea. Be a good girl for Aunty Mary."

Thea didn't answer; she pretended not to hear, but she watched from behind the curtain as Mabel walked along the path and got into a waiting car. Mary, dressed in a cream linen dress, was standing by the gate waving until the car was out of sight.

Over two months had passed since that day and she had settled in well with her aunt and uncle. As she sat sewing, leaning against her aunt's leg, she felt that she had lived with her aunt for ages and ages and the picture of Hacketts Cottage was far less clear in her mind. The time before Hacketts Cottage she had to struggle desperately to recall, and as a baby no memory at all.

"Where was I born?" asked Thea.

Mary, lifting her head from her sewing, looked into her niece's questioning eyes. "Birmingham. In a nursing home in Birmingham," she said.

"Oh!" replied the child thoughtfully, still looking into her aunt's gentle face. "Did you see me when I was a baby?"

"Yes, I did. Do you know," said Mary, "I saw you when you were a day old. You were only so big."

She held out her hands to show the child the size of a baby. "You were a dear little thing, all snuggled down in a crib."

"Was I pretty?" Came the enquiry.

"You were very nice indeed," said Mary. "All rounded, pink and cuddly. I remember the day so well when I first saw you. I had phoned the nursing home to learn that you had been born just an hour before."

"What day was it?" asked Thea.

"Saturday," came the reply. "Saturday evening. The saying goes that 'Saturday's Child works hard for her living'. I wonder if that will be true of you?"

"Isn't Saturday a very good day to be born on, then?" questioned

Thea. Then a little querulously she added, "Shouldn't a person be born on a Saturday?"

"It's just a saying," said Mary. "I am sure it makes no difference at all."

"What do you think the best day to be born on is?" said Thea, placing her hands on her aunt's knees, while looking up at her in innocent curiosity.

"Sunday, most definitely Sunday," replied Mary.

Thea stopped her sewing and thoughtfully scratched white marks on her arm with the eye of her needle. "Tell me about when you first saw me. Tell me all about myself," she said.

"Well, let me think," said Mary, taking off her sewing glasses and brushing her hair away from her face. "It was about eight o'clock in the evening when I phoned the nursing home, and I decided to visit your mother the next day. It was a hot spell of weather, rather like it is today, but much more humid. There was quite a bad storm on the evening you were born and I remember how miserable I felt and how heavy the atmosphere was, full of omens somehow."

"Full of omens?" enquired the child. "What are omens?"

"Thoughts and feelings for the future," said Mary. "Your future, your mother's future, the future of the family."

Thea pondered on the word future and what it really meant in relationship to her as a tiny baby. She tried to imagine herself small and pink in a crib, as a beloved possession.

"The next morning," said Mary, "I caught the train to Birmingham. It was a clear sparkling morning, washed clean from the overnight storms. I remember how I stood waiting on the station feeling very apprehensive and nervous, hoping that no one would ask me where I was going."

"Why?" said Thea. "You could have told them you were going to see the baby that had just been born."

"No one knew you had been born, only me. Of our family and friends, only I knew you had been born." Mary spoke softly and looked at the child with concern.

"Why was I a secret?" said the child with a great surge of dismay.

"Well, my darling, you were a secret. You'll understand as you get older, but don't bother your head about it now." Mary spoke gently as she stroked Thea's head. Changing the subject, she said, "Do you know the hot sun has lightened your hair, made it go quite golden in places."

Thea, puzzled by the secrecy said, "How did I get to Mammy's then?"

Mary hesitated for a few minutes, fiddling with the buttons on the front of her dress before replying softly, "I handed you over to Mrs Clements in the middle of Worcester bridge."

"Why on the bridge?" asked Thea, with a sudden picture of Worcester bridge and the river, flooding into her mind. "How did Mammy know to be on the bridge?"

"Your mother made the arrangements—it wasn't my idea." Mary looked at the child sadly. "I didn't think it was a good idea, but Mabel said it was, so I was given the job of handing you over to Mrs Clements for her to look after you."

Thea, scratching at a scab on her knee said, "If Mabel is my mother, why did I go to Mammy, and why haven't I got a Dad."

Mary patted Thea's head, "Don't worry about it my dear, don't even think about it."

Thea knew that there was a lot of things she hadn't got, but it was the first time she had ever said the word 'Dad', and it frightened her with its intensity and implications. "Did Granny know I was born?" she blurted out, suddenly longing for some one close to her to be pleased that she was born.

Thea turned to her aunt and smiled, just a quick flash of radiance, and said, "Shall I always be here?"

"I should imagine so, unless your mother wants you to live with her some time." Mary held her hands out towards her niece. "We must always remember that you are Mabel's little girl. You know when you were born, your mother didn't want to have you adopted, she said, 'No, I can't give her away, she belongs to the family, we must keep her.' Your mother was crying so bitterly she didn't know what to do, but I wanted her to keep you too, and so here you are with us. I am pleased you are here with us."

Thea had enjoyed the time she had been with her aunt and uncle because she had begun to feel loved just for herself. The house and garden were peaceful and beautiful, and no harsh words tore at the atmosphere or bruised the delicate fibre of her being. She knew her aunt loved her, but she felt disturbed and frightened because of their recent conversation. For a second or two she felt transported back to Hacketts Cottage, a place that she hadn't thought of for weeks, and she burst out almost compulsively, "Shall we go and see Mammy and the others?"

Momentarily Mary looked startled and said with great apprehension in her voice, "Why, Thea, do you want to go back to Mrs Clements?"

Noticing the tension in her aunt's face, Thea said, "I didn't say goodbye to any of them. They must wonder where I am. I would like to stay here, but I ought to say goodbye to Mammy." She moved across and sat down against her aunt's knee, and tried laboriously to put the cotton back through the eye of the needle.

"We will see what we can do to arrange a visit, if that will please you," said Mary, taking the needle from the child's hand and threading the cotton through it.

During the time that Thea had lived with her aunt and uncle she had put on weight, and her arms and legs were plumper. Freckles sprinkled her nose and she had grown out of her shoes. One village school had been exchanged for another, but the set-up of the schools was so similar that she had not had to suffer any great changes.

A mile or so to school was walked in the company of Jenny, the farmer's youngest daughter. She was a lively, extrovert, good-looking girl about a year older than Thea. She protected Thea from the bullies and the louts who lurked in the lanes, for not only was she strong and lively but she had four grown-up brothers—as well as two sisters—and they were admired generally in the locality.

The brothers were all strong, muscular, fair-haired and good-looking, being the heroes of the small boys. When the sun shone, they worked around the farm just in trousers and shoes, their torsos glistening, golden brown.

Thea loved to play with Jenny around the farm, chasing in and out of the large barns, and sliding down the yellow bales of hay. Brother Joe showed the girls how to feed the young calves who had been separated from their mothers by putting their hands in the buckets of milk and letting the fingers go upwards, so that the soft-mouthed creatures could suck the milk through their fingers.

The brothers had infinite patience and seemed happy to have the little girls with them when they went hay-making, allowing them to ride on the wagons and jump and leap in the sweet smelling, flower scented hay.

Visiting Granny, too, was always a pleasure for Thea, being particularly enjoyable as she was allowed to go on her own. During the summer holidays scarcely a day passed when the way was not traversed either by Thea alone, or with her aunt, or by Granny walking in the opposite direction. Thea particularly liked to spend time with Granny on her own, for she loved the gentle, understanding, elderly lady, whose voice was always soft and whose patience for explaining things knew no bounds.

Granny played the piano, enjoyed painting pictures, loved poetry and would read endless stories to Thea with obvious pleasure. She would take the child walking through the woods and meadows explaining to her all the time the names of the wild flowers, the trees and the birds. Under her grandmother's guidance and her aunt's sensitivity and love, Thea grew physically and mentally like a plant which has suddenly found itself in the right soil and climate.

Warm summer afternoons would often find Thea sprawled out on the grass under the pear tree in her granny's garden with books she had been allowed to choose from the book-case. Granny would sit in her wicker chair, and a beautiful rapport would flow between the older lady and the child, so that the hours seemed to be golden and suspended. Stories of childhood were told again to receptive ears, and occasions sparkled bright and new in the child's eyes.

"Tell me about when you were a little girl, Gran," the voice would lift expectantly over the scented bushes and flowers.

"I was born at an inn on the Cotswolds, the youngest of the family. My mother supervised the running of the pub and the brewing of the ale, but my father worked away a lot of the time as a clerk to a circuit judge. My older sister was twenty when I was born. Then there were three brothers that I knew, although there had been twin boys who had died, and then me, the baby of the family."

"Did you like being the baby, Gran?" asked Thea, already transported to the inn in some distant Cotswold town.

"I was spoilt, I suppose, very much fussed over by my father. He expected great things of the boys, but he only wanted me to be pretty and good. I went to school, but I was taught really 'how to be

a lady', that was considered the most important thing in life: to be
refined and elegant, so to be eligible for marriage. I sewed, painted,
sang, played the piano, learnt to walk correctly, speak beautifully of
course, and know how to be a successful hostess."

"Were you beautiful, Granny?"

"Just ordinary, I should imagine, my darling. I had brown hair
like you, only it was very long, so long I could sit on it. My eyes
were grey, well they still are of course, but they have gone a bit
faded. I was a small girl, never got to be more than five feet tall."

"Did Grandpa fall instantly in love with you?" enquired the child.

With a little chuckle the old lady said almost girlishly, "I thought
he was very handsome. He rode a large chestnut horse and I
admired him tremendously long before I was ever introduced to
him."

"What was he like, Gran?"

"Oh, tall, slender and very dark."

"And so you married him and lived happily ever after," said Thea
happily.

Granny, looking wistful, thoughtfully strained her silk dress over
her knees. "Things don't always turn out as you expect," she said.
"We married about three years later, and during the next three
years Mary, Mabel and Margaret were born. And then a series of
misfortunes befell your grandfather and he altered. Well, my dear,
don't worry your pretty head about such things."

She loved to chat with her grandmother and now felt part of a
large family, although she had met only a few of its members.
However, when her grandmother spoke she felt that she knew
everyone. Granny's garden was a magical place for a small girl.
Paths twisted round rhododendron bushes and the shrubbery was
an enchanted cool paradise. There were rose bushes, lavender
hedges and brilliant herbaceous borders. Every morning an elderly
man helped in the garden. He dug, puffed, weeded and rubbed his
back in the most melancholy manner.

He hardly ever spoke, and never smiled, but in spite of his moans
and creaking bones, produced vegetables of enormous proportions
and blooms of flower show extravagance. He was a wizened little
man with a hooked nose and pale watery eyes. No one had ever
seen him without his trilby hat, which was always well pulled down

over his ears. He wore an old brown twill cow-gown tied round the middle with a thick piece of string. He nurtured a great suspicion for all things human, especially young humans.

One morning Mary announced to Thea that she would be spending the day with Evelyn Booth, a friend of hers. This surprised the child, for although Miss Booth was a frequent visitor to the house, to spend a day with her was most unexpected.

As she went to the bathroom to get washed her aunt said brightly, "You are spending the day with Miss Booth, so put on your Hungarian dress."

"Where are we going?" called Thea excitedly. "Is Uncle Robert coming too?"

"No, only you," said Mary. "Aren't you lucky, just imagine, a whole day on your own with Miss Booth."

Something in her aunt's voice sharpened Thea's senses, making her feel immediately that there was some underlying reason for her spending the day with Miss Booth. She had never been out with Miss Booth on her own before, so she was particularly puzzled by the arrangement.

"Why just me?" she asked, as she squeezed the flannel dripping with water, allowing the water to run up her arms. "Why aren't you coming? What are you going to do?"

"I have an elderly aunt coming to visit. She and Granny will be coming to lunch," said Mary.

A rebellious surge swept through her body, she felt that her aunt was trying to get her out of the house for the day. "I want to have lunch with you," she blurted out. "I want to have lunch with you and Granny. I don't want to go with Miss Booth."

Mary entered the bathroom and said soothingly, "But you like Miss Booth, and she is very fond of you. It has all been arranged, so you are going to be a good girl and have a pleasant day with Miss Booth."

Thea threw the flannel into the basin full of water with such force that the water splashed up the wall violently cascading on to the lino. She knew that she was being got out of the house purposely, that her day out with Miss Booth had not been arranged as a treat.

"Stop it, Thea," demanded Mary sharply. "You are going to do as you are told. Now wash your neck, stop being silly and try to be a good girl."

Thea splashed the water over her face, grabbed the towel and turned towards her aunt, who was sitting on the edge of the bath watching her. "Why can't I have lunch with you and Granny?"

"Because, my darling, Aunt Julia is very difficult," she replied.

"Who is Aunt Julia?" Thea asked, her voice quivering on the verge of tears. She stood, a small defiant figure in her underwear, holding a large white towel to her chest and neck.

Mary put her arms around the child's thin shoulders. "Be good, darling," she pleaded. "Aunt Julia is Granny's sister-in-law, and she doesn't know that you have been born. We feel it is best if she doesn't know."

She wriggled away from her aunt and ran into the bedroom, grabbing her teddy for comfort. She couldn't understand how people could say that they loved her but be ashamed of her at the same time. Granny told her all about the family, but there were obviously members of the family who didn't know she had been born: she found it very puzzling.

Looking at herself in the dressing table mirror, she gazed at her reflection to see what was wrong with herself, and why it was that Aunt Julia mustn't see her. She was sure that she looked quite normal and wasn't ugly or terrible in any way. She climbed on to the window-sill, sitting the teddy bear up on her knees. He looked at her compassionately through his odd coloured eyes, as though he knew exactly how she felt. She kissed his almost threadbare head, smelling his sweet straw dusty smell, and whispered into his inanimate ear, "I love you more than anything in the world, for you are my friend."

"Hurry up Thea, put on your Hungarian dress." Aunty Mary's voice cut through her thoughts. She jumped off the window-sill and walked across to the wardrobe to get her embroidered dress.

When Miss Booth arrived she was so full of sparkling good humour that Thea soon put her disagreeable feelings aside. It was a perfect September day, and once on the hills Miss Booth took off her high-heeled shoes and raced bare-foot with Thea along the soft grass of the ridges. The wind ruffled their hair and brought roses to their cheeks, and gave them an appetite for the goodies that were being carried in the rucksack on Miss Booth's back. In the afternoon they went to the Lanchester Marionette Theatre in Malvern, gasping at the cleverness of the puppeteer, and then had tea in the Dorothy Cafe in Church Street.

As they walked back to Aunty Mary's house, a soft mist lay in the hollows on the common, and the air smelt slightly damp and heavy with the odour of the later summer flowers. A pale silver moon was visible in the sky.

"We must turn our money and make a wish," said Miss Booth. Together they stood by the gate laughing, making their wishes while their sixpences turned in their hands.

One mid-September morning, when the air was hanging with mist and spiders' webs were transformed to lace, Thea and Jenny were walking along the lanes to school. Jenny was strangely quiet. She seemed to drag her feet and had no enthusiasm for anything. Just before reaching school she was violently sick. She sat on the grass verge by the side of the road shivering and looking pale.

Thea didn't know what to do to help her friend. "I will take you back home, Jenny," she said. "You had better go home."

Jenny, shaking her head, said, "It will pass. I expect it is something I have eaten."

The teacher at school seemed very concerned when she saw Jenny, insisting that she lie in the armchair in her study by the window. She gave her a glass of cold water and told her to close her eyes and see if that would help the sickness to pass. However it didn't pass, and in the middle of the morning the gardener was despatched on his bicycle to get one of the family to fetch her home. Brother Joe, dusty and straw-covered from threshing in the farmyard, drove to the school to collect his little sister. The children watched from the classroom window as he carried her out to the car, placing her tenderly in the back seat.

Thea ran along the lanes after school, eager to get home and tell her aunt about Jenny. She burst into the hallway, hot and breathless, shouting, "Aunty Mary, Aunty Mary, Jenny is ill. She was sick and Joe had to take her home."

"Why have you run all the way home?" said Mary, coming out of the kitchen in response to the noise. "Look how hot you are, you silly little girl."

"Jenny is ill," blurted out Thea. "She had to go home—she was sick."

"Now come along, wash your face and cool down. Then go across to the farm and ask how Jenny is," said Mary, lifting the satchel from her niece's back. "I am sure she will be better. I expect her mother put her to bed."

Thea did as her aunt suggested as quickly as possible and hurried across to the farm. The warm afternoon sun was mellow and golden as she walked along the gravel driveway to the farm which was flanked by chestnut trees that had already begun to shed their shining conkers. The farm geese strutted heavily around, one or two stretching out their necks in half-hearted fashion at Thea, and a gander sat on the grass at the front of the house, blinking his bright blue eyes in the sun.

Jenny's brother Gerald answered the door and looked grave as he said, "Mum and Dad are at the hospital with Jenny. She has got to have an operation."

Thea didn't know what to say, so she just stood in the large doorway looking up at Gerald.

"I expect they will come home when the operation is over, but I just don't know," said Gerald, rubbing his chin. "We didn't expect that she would have to have an operation."

Thea turned away in dismay, not really comprehending what Gerald's news meant, but realising that it was serious because of his attitude.

Aunty Mary was in the garden as Thea walked back over the common. "Is she better darling?" she called.

Thea shook her head. "No, Gerald said she is in hospital, she has had an operation."

"Oh dear," Mary stood with the scissors in one hand and a bunch of bronze chrysanthemums in the other. "How dreadful. Poor little Jenny."

It wasn't until the late afternoon of the following day that further news was received of Jenny. Nora, the oldest girl of the family, called to say that her sister was very ill; the appendix had burst, and she had peritonitis. The surgeon felt that her condition was very serious indeed. On the posting outside the hospital, she was on the 'Very Poorly' list. Having delivered the news, she burst into tears.

Mary comforted her and made her sit down and have a cup of tea. "I can't understand how it got as far as bursting. Didn't she have any symptoms before yesterday when she was sick?"

Nora's face was blotched with crying, her eyes red and swollen. She looked up at Mary shaking her head. "A little tummy ache from time to time, but we thought it was because she had been eating too many apples. We never dreamt that it was the appendix getting inflamed."

Robert came in from work and was told the news. Looking very distressed he said, "Tummy ache should never be ignored. I doubt whether the child will pull through. Peritonitis is severe blood poisoning; a very bad thing, very bad."

Thea went to her room and lay on her bed sobbing for her friend. It was unbelievable to think of Jenny as ill. Lovely, active Jenny. Surely God couldn't let her die, He wouldn't be so cruel.

On the evening of the next day Jenny died. Gerald was returning from the hospital as Robert was walking back over the common. He stopped the car, pulled down the window, and said, "She is gone."

Robert repeated the incident when he sat down to tea. "The child has died," he said quietly. "The family are devastated. Such a terrible waste of a young life, a dreadful, dreadful thing. Gerald told me; he was crying bitterly. I should imagine the mother will never recover from the shock. A dreadful thing."

When the children gathered at the village school on the Monday morning, everyone knew of Jenny's death. Death seemed to have sprung with unreasonable viciousness and caught in its net a healthy and well-liked child. The grown-ups, stunned by the suddenness of it all, realised that any of the children could have been chosen to die in such a fashion and feeling especially protective, several mothers had accompanied their offspring to school.

Thea walked with Roland, a boy who lived with his grandmother in a cottage a short way along the lane. In ordinary circumstances she would have been a little afraid of Roland, for he was loud-mouthed and fat and took a fiendish delight in pushing girls into muddy ditches. However, on that particular morning he looked subdued and was standing by the gate with his grandmother, and as Thea came level with the gate, he started to walk by the side of her, hands stuffed in his pockets, head down, kicking the gravel of the lane with his heavy boots.

Miss Taylor, solemn-faced and pale, grouped the children together, as was customary, into the large classroom for morning prayers. Squeezing a handkerchief in her hand, she said with a voice filled with emotion, "This is going to be difficult for all of us, very difficult. We will all close our eyes and pray." At this point emotion overcame her and she was unable to speak. Tears poured down her cheeks and a terrible silence filled the room, for never before had the children seen this figure of authority in any way upset, let alone crying. A young teacher, who taught the infants, stepped forward and quietly said, "We will pray for the family of Jenny, as Miss Taylor said. We will pray in silence, each in our own way."

United in communal sorrow, the children stood in a heavy silence which was broken only by the odd sniff and the harsh breathing coming from restricted throats. The only movement was the occasional sleeve which was raised to wipe a dripping nose. After a few minutes the young teacher read Psalm 23, after which Miss Taylor seemed more herself, and was able to speak to the children.

"Tomorrow Jenny will be buried, and I think it would be nice if you each brought a few flowers, your own small token of remembrance." She looked up at the children, her eyes moist and pink. "We will have our own little service after the family have gone. We mustn't intrude into their grief."

The next morning the children found it hard not to keep glancing through the windows at the line of black cars and the sorrowing brothers carrying the body of their little sister into church.

When the family had gone and the churchyard was empty, the children quietly lined up, each with their own token. They crossed the lane, and gathering round the small flower covered mound under the yew tree, and added their own flowers.

Chapter Five

THEA loved the church which was close to the cottage where they lived, and happily each Sunday she accompanied her aunt and uncle there for morning service. She was fascinated by the dark red Victorian murals which covered the walls, and would try to work out which stories from the Bible they were meant to represent. She knew the story of Noah's Ark, and Moses and the Bulrushes, and Ruth and the Corn, but she couldn't recognise them from the figures on the wall.

Uncle Robert was a sidesman and collected the money during the last hymn, but always very keen to tell people that he had sung for most of his life in the church choir. Thea often wondered what the vicar did with the money once it was taken up to the altar and blessed. She supposed that God slipped down quietly after the service and took it back with Him to heaven.

There were almshouses attached to the church, and Thea sometimes went into their large communal garden and chatted to the old people. At the far end of the garden was a wrought iron gate which led across a meadow to a stream and a wood. She would go there with a jam pot and try and catch minnows, but their silvery quickness evaded her more often than not, so that all she would take home would be a solitary fresh water shrimp.

Thea often accompanied her grandmother when she tended the grave in the churchyard. She would fetch the water that stood in large barrels by the gateway and take it to her grandmother, so that she could fill the green flower containers. She would take the dead flowers, placing them on the rubbish pile against the hedge, where flies resting in the warmth of the decaying heap would rise in the air in an angry buzz when more dead flowers with slimy stems were thrown on.

She would watch patiently while her grandmother knelt down and cut the grass on the grave with shears. She was particularly fascinated when the stone cross was erected which said, 'In Loving memory of Frederick William, Beloved Husband'. She accepted with unquestioning childlike faith that the white haired old gentleman that she got to know at Christmas time was lying in the earth asleep and yet at the same time with Jesus in heaven.

"He was a good man when he was younger," Granny would say, cutting away at the grass. "No one could have had a kinder husband, but a sort of weakness crept in as he got older. I don't think he could help himself, and it is wrong to speak ill of the dead, but he lacked a strength of character in some ways."

"What was his weakness, Gran?" Thea asked time and time again. "How was he weak?"

Granny would sigh and say, "Pretty faces and drink, those were his weaknesses."

Not understanding the implications of the statement, Thea would puzzle on how a pretty face or a drink could be a weakness, but then grown-ups frequently made odd and puzzling statements that seemed to bear no relevance to everyday life. Aunty Mary had told her that Grandfather had lost a lot of money over a lawsuit involving land, and that foot and mouth disease and swine fever had swept through his model farm, so he had to have all the animals destroyed.

The two shocks had occurred at much the same time, and he hadn't been able to cope with the misfortunes. Aunty Mary concluded that because he had been spoilt by his parents, he hadn't got the strength of character to fight back when life pushed him down. He was an only son, so very much indulged; that might have affected him, but so might the fact that he was sent away to school at a very early age, Aunty Mary confided.

Whatever the reason for Grandfather's weaknesses, Thea felt that she should remember him and that is why she gladly accompanied her grandmother when she performed the ritual of attending the grave.

The elderly people who lived in the almshouses seemed to derive a certain amount of pleasure from the presence of the child playing in their garden. They would watch her easy movements as she skipped and danced on the grass and between the flower beds. She felt that the garden was in some way special and secret, and she frequently seemed unaware that the old people could see her as she worked out her dances and make-believe games. Sometimes she would sit in one or other of the porchways and listen to the accounts of when they were young, and the stories they told seemed as far away and as fantastic as if they had stepped from the pages of Hans Christian Andersen.

Isabelle was going to be eight at the end of October, and Thea had received an invitation to her birthday party. A car was being sent to collect her at about two o'clock, and she would be returned during the early evening. She felt overwhelmingly happy to think that Isabelle should have included her, and she looked forward with delightful anticipation to the occasion.

On the appointed day, at the agreed time, she was ready, dressed in a new holly green velvet dress, hair curled and tied up in green ribbons, and carrying the birthday present under her arm. She climbed into the back seat of the chauffeur-driven car, feeling very grand as she waved Aunty Mary goodbye.

Thea and her family lived about forty minutes' car drive away, and as the party was to begin at three o'clock, Thea arrived at the house with time to spare. During the drive, the chauffeur, a jolly, fatherly sort of man, had chatted away, which made the journey slip by quickly.

The car had hardly pulled to a halt when Isabelle and Gloria came rushing down the steps from the front door, calling and waving excitedly. They were dressed alike in pale blue dresses, and as the wind tossed their flaxen curls, they looked even prettier than Thea had remembered. Their mother stood on the top of the steps holding the collar of the Red Setter dog to stop him jumping up against the girls' dresses.

"Put him in the stable Monty," she called to the chauffeur. "He is such a devil jumping up and barking, he will frighten some of the little girls."

The chauffeur took the dog whose boisterous enthusiasm nearly pulled the man off his feet, and made off towards the back of the house. Isabelle and Gloria held Thea's free hand and led her up the steps and into the house, while Rosemary, the mother of Isabelle and Gloria, kissed her and told her how pretty she looked.

Like all little girls in new dresses, Thea felt beautiful and she was wonderfully happy to be with Isabelle; even though she was a little older, she felt a warmth and closeness to her. She knew Isabelle liked her, which was the most important thing in the world, so with joy she handed over the birthday present, hoping that it was what her friend would like.

"We'll undo it in the drawing room," said Isabelle. "Daddy is in there and you haven't met him."

The three girls walked across the large, light hall and through the open door into the drawing room which was flooded with warm, October afternoon sunshine. It was a large room with French windows opening on to the garden from a round bay. A tall, fair-haired man stood by the open window, smoking a pipe, and he turned and smiled at the children. He was dressed ready for golf in plus-fours and a tweedy jacket, which made him look even bigger than he was.

"Friends here already!" he exclaimed. "I thought I would have made my escape before the invasion.." He laughed good humour-edly and walked across to the sofa to see the present.

"It's Thea," said Isabelle. "She has come a little earlier, as the car had to fetch her." She began to undo the ribbon from round the present with Gloria's eager fingers trying desperately to help. The younger girl began to jump excitedly up and down on the sofa until her father lifted her firmly off and told her to calm down.

The gift was a small loom with a selection of coloured wools, which Isabelle was genuinely pleased with, exclaiming that it was just what she wanted. Her father seemed very interested and read the instructions carefully, announcing that he would help Isabelle set up the loom when the party was over, and he was back from his round of golf.

Thea had never met a man like the girls' father. He seemed so handsome, charming and friendly that he appeared to belong to a different race of men than those that she was used to. Never having had a father, she hadn't a model with which to compare other men. Tom and Uncle Robert were the only men that she really knew, and Uncle Robert, being a quiet, retiring sort of person, was in no way colourful or given to extremes. True he was always kind to Thea, and would talk or play sensible games with her, but he bore no comparison to this attractive smiling fair-haired giant of a man.

To Thea, Isabelle and Gloria had everything that anyone could wish for, for not only were they pretty, but they had an attractive vivacious mother, a handsome father, and lived in a lovely house. In addition to that, they had ponies of their own and a red setter dog.

When the doorbell rang, the girls' father wished them goodbye, calling "I'm going darling, best of luck" to his wife, grabbed his golf bag, stepped out through the French windows and strode across the garden.

Isabelle and Gloria had gone with their mother to greet newly arriving guests. Thea stood in the doorway to the garden watching the disappearing figure of their father. A gate opened from the bottom of the garden on to the golf course, so the house was conveniently situated to combine home life with what was his favourite leisure activity. Late summer roses soaked in the autumn sunshine, Michaelmas daisies vibrated with bees and a flamboyant patch of nasturtiums crawled across the crazy paving of the terrace. Excited voices shrilled from the hall, while in the distance the imprisoned dog could be heard barking frustratedly. The girls' mother came into the room, followed by her sister Penelope, the mother of Angela and Stella. Penelope looked towards the open windows, saw Thea and her features immediately changed.

"Rosemary, what are you playing at?" she hissed at her sister, her eyes blazing with indignation.

"Isabelle's friend, she wanted it," Rosemary answered, almost defensively, glancing nervously in Thea's direction.

Penelope's face was ashen and her voice trembled as she turned towards her sister and said, "I think you are a traitor. have you no feeling for your sister-in-law? I can't understand you."

"Please, Penelope, don't make a scene," Rosemary pleaded. "Anyhow, think of the child. You are not being very kind."

"Think of the child! Why the hell should I think of the child? Think of your own family!" Penelope retorted, flinging herself with emotion into one of the chairs. "If you are thinking of repeating the performance, perhaps you would have the decency to inform me first, then the girls and I won't bother to come." Her voice trembled but cut like a cold draught across the warmth of the afternoon.

Thea knew that she was somehow to blame for the outburst, but she couldn't think what she had done wrong, being even more puzzled to know why Penelope disliked her so. She suddenly felt very afraid, for the knowledge that she was in some obscure way responsible for the anger of the woman hit her like an awareness of

pain. She slipped through the window and crouched, almost paralysed with apprehension, on the terrace against the wall, where she
couldn't be seen from the drawing room. She had never heard
women raise their voices to each other, and it was in every way
more terrible than Mammy and Tom arguing, which she had grown
to accept as an everyday occurrence.

"Pen, sometimes you are such a bitch," said Rosemary hoarsely.
"Mother accepts, why can't you?"

"Mother!" Penelope almost snorted. "Mother will cling to anything that she feels remotely belongs to her. She loves possessing
things, and at times I feel she has no moral values."

Thea slipped round the corner from the terrace, and went
towards the potting shed. No longer could she hear the women's
voices, but the sound of laughing children echoed through the open
doorway and windows, but she didn't know how to join them. The
day was spoilt for her and she stood rejected and abandoned in the
long grass behind the potting shed. The smell of compost, heavy
with a rotting sweetness, pervaded the air, and the nettles standing
fiercely in their dried greenness exuded the characteristic odour of
decay that vegetation gives off in autumn.

It seemed to Thea that she had stood there for a very long time
when her misery was interrupted by a voice calling her name. It was
Nanny Davis, her voice floating over the garden with a shrill
urgency. "Thea, Thea, where are you? The girls are looking for
you. Come along, where are you hiding?"

Thea decided that she would behave quite normally, pretending
that she had been walking in the garden while Isabelle was greeting
her friends. "I'm here," she said, stepping out through the long
grass. "I've only been waiting for Isabelle."

"We've been looking all over for you," exclaimed Nanny Davis,
with a puzzled expression on her face. "Isabelle said you were in the
drawing room, we have looked all over the house. We didn't think
that you would be in the garden."

Nanny Davis held Thea's hand as they walked towards the
French windows of the drawing room. Only Angela was in the
drawing room looking at Isabelle's cards which had been arranged
along the mantelpiece and on several side tables. She glanced
towards them as they entered the room; she didn't speak, but

picked up a card and began to read it, as though the nanny and child were of no consequence to her, and certainly not worth the effort of an acknowledgement.

"We are going to watch the conjuror," said Nanny. "Are you coming, Angela?" Nanny paused in the doorway to the hall and looked at Angela questioningly.

Angela looked up and her expression was cool and aloof. "I might," she said in an off-hand way, "but I'm really here to help control them at tea." She put an emphasis on them, which suggested that she thought the younger girls to be far inferior to her. "Stella might like to watch," she added, turning her back and continuing to pick up the cards and examine them.

Nanny Davis made an impatient clicking noise with her mouth, as she and Thea went upstairs into the day nursery to join the other guests for the conjuring show. The little girls were sitting in a bright, expectant group waiting for the conjuror to begin his magic, and as Thea entered the room Isabelle let out a great whoop of delight.

"Oh, there you are, Thea. We thought you had got lost," she shrieked. "Come and sit by me. Look everyone, this is Thea, my very best friend."

Isabelle's words did something to ease Thea's bruised feelings, so she sat and leaned against her young friend with a feeling of gratitude and relief. After some time she began to laugh with the rest, forgetting for a while the unpleasant episode of the afternoon. Even Stella, who had been sitting on the window-sill in the room, there but apart from the company, began to laugh and at one time she even jumped from her perch and began to clap appreciatively. Angela slipped into the room almost unnoticed for the last five minutes of the entertainment, leaning against the wall with a half smile playing on her lips.

After tea, Nanny Davis and Isabelle's and Gloria's mother arranged some games which took place in the drawing room. Penelope sat quietly in a chair watching, the anger of the earlier part of the afternoon appearing to have subsided, while Angela and Stella helped with the giving out of paper and pencils and arranging blindfolds.

In no time at all the party was over. Nannies called for their charges and Thea found herself in the car being driven back home.

She felt strangely tired, as though the events and excitement of the afternoon had drained all her strength and energy. She leaned back in the seat, watching through half closed eyes the trees and fields lurch by in the gathering gloom of the October evening.

Just before going to bed, Thea sat by the fire with Aunty Mary. "What's a traitor?" she asked innocently.

"Oh, a very nasty person," replied Mary. "One who betrays, lets down. In fact a person who goes against everything that is good and honourable. Why do you ask, darling?"

"Well, Angela and Stella's mother, Isabelle's Aunty Penelope, called Isabelle's mother a traitor because she had invited me to Isabelle's party," said Thea, looking up into her aunt's face. "I don't think she likes me."

Aunty Mary's reaction was immediate and volatile. "That finishes it. You will never go there again," she said, rising from her chair and throwing her knitting on to the cushion that she had just vacated. "How dare she speak like that! Who does she think she is? I shall tell your mother that you are to have nothing to do with those people."

Robert, who was writing at his desk in the corner of the room, looked up and with a surprised intonation in his voice said, "What on earth is the matter, Mary?"

"Those wretched people, saying unkind things about Thea, to such an extent that she knew and understood," said Mary tensely. "I find it quite unbelievable and absolutely intolerable."

Thea leant against the fire-guard quite puzzled by her aunt's attitude, for she seemed so cross and flustered. "She didn't say anything to me," volunteered Thea. "She called Rosemary a traitor."

"Just the same," snapped Mary, clenching her fists and pacing across the room.

Robert, his voice calm and placating, said, "I'm not surprised, Mary. I felt it was very unwise to let the child go in the first place. I personally think it's better to have nothing to do with them."

A great feeling of dismay swept through Thea's small body, for she liked Isabelle and Gloria and their parents. She also liked her godmother. She felt confused and alarmed that her presence caused people to react and quarrel with each other. She couldn't understand what it was about her that sent ripples of discord across the surface of otherwise calm waters.

"Well, we know where we stand now," said Mary. "The incident is passed. We shall not mention it again. Come along, Thea, time for bed."

She held her hand out towards the child and led her upstairs to bed. "You must be tired," she said softly, "It's been a very busy day."

Washed and cosy in pink winceyette pyjamas, Thea snuggled between the sheets. Mary bent down to kiss her but before she did she stroked the child's forehead and hair gently. "Go to sleep, my darling, don't worry about anything. Your guardian angel will take care of you."

"Where is my guardian angel?" enquired Thea nervously.

"At the foot of your bed, of course," said Mary, adjusting the night–light holder. "No harm will come to you while you have a guardian angel."

She stepped from the room pulling the bedroom door quietly behind her. The bedroom window was open slightly and the curtains moved gently. The shadows made by the nightlight began to leap and dance across the walls. Thea didn't shut her eyes but watched the frightening movements and shapes.

She was afraid of the dark, but only a little less terrified of the night–light gloom and the awful dancing shadows. Aunty Mary mentioning the angel seemed to make the room more terrible, as its presence didn't bring reassurance but rather a feeling of foreboding. Aunty Maud, Uncle Robert's sister, had two pictures of angels, but to Thea they were not comforting pictures.

One showed a little girl leaning across water to pick some flowers with the angel behind her trying to prevent her slipping, and the other was of a small boy walking across a rotten wooden bridge with the angel behind trying to guide his steps before the bridge collapsed completely. The grown–ups seemed to talk about the pictures as if they were beautiful reminders of the goodness of God, and how He sent His angels to guard everyone on earth. It did occur to Thea that sometimes the angels weren't very conscientious about their duties because accidents and deaths did happen, such as Jenny. At the thought of Jenny a cold feeling vibrated down Thea's spine and tears stung her eyes.

Thea looked at the moving shadows on the wall at the foot of her bed and quite easily she could see the figure of an angel. Its wings moved gently with the movement of the curtains and its eyes were fixed in a threatening gaze, looking directly at her.

"Please, please go back to heaven," whispered Thea quietly. "I'm all right, really I am. Please go and look after someone else."

The angel didn't move but went on swaying its wings in the same manner, keeping the same expression on its face, which made her cry out in terror. The angel took no notice and the shadows continued to flicker and dance in dark, distorted shapes. She called out more loudly and urgently until her calls became continuous, hysterical screams.

Mary and Robert came bounding up the stairs, convinced that the child must be on fire or that some other terrible accident had befallen her. "What's wrong? What's wrong?" gasped Mary, rushing into the room with Robert close behind her. She moved towards the bed and grasped the screaming, trembling child.

"The angel," sobbed Thea. "Tell the angel to go away. I don't want it on the bottom of my bed. Tell the angel that I shall be all right."

Robert's voice broke into the confusion, calm and authoritative. "Angel, please go away," he commanded. He then picked up Thea from her aunt's arms, saying quite firmly, "There is no one in this room except you and me and Aunty Mary. Look, you can see the room is empty."

He carried the child in his arms showing her every corner of the room. "Now you are going back to bed and this time you are going to sleep," he said.

Putting the child on the bed, he left his wife to tuck her in, while he walked over to the window, closed it firmly and, moving the night-light on to a table on the landing, left the faintest light to glow through the open doorway.

It was the Saturday before Christmas when Mary decided to take Thea to visit Mrs Clements. The day was grey and miserable with a hint of snow in the atmosphere, and from the bus window the fields looked drab and desolate. The bony shapes of the naked trees leered in the greyness and those in the distance were wrapped in a shroud of mist.

Thea felt excited, yet strangely apprehensive, as her aunt was uncommonly quiet and subdued. She had promised to take her niece to her former foster mother, so she was sticking to her word, although somewhat reluctantly. In her heart there was the fear that the child might prefer the cosy muddle of Hacketts Cottage and the companionship of the other children to her own quiet, well-run home and her rather conservative husband. The child had brought a happiness and sparkle to their lives and she dreaded the light being extinguished.

The day before she had taken Thea to buy presents for the Clements and the children who lived with them and they had had great fun choosing suitable gifts. They had purchased a pink hand-knitted bed jacket for Mammy; a tobacco pouch and tobacco for Tom; scented soap and a box of embroidered handkerchiefs for Marjory; a Dutch doll in a pretty check dress for Monica; a book on aeroplanes for Vince; and a smart tie with a tie-pin for Laurence. They had bought boxes of chocolates and sweets to share around and also to have something in hand in case other children should be at Hacketts Cottage for Christmas.

The gifts were wrapped in red and green Christmas paper and were sitting splendidly in a large basket on the bus seat by the side of them. They jumped a little in the basket as the bus rattled over some of the uneven surfaces of the lanes.

"I am sure Mammy will be ever so pleased to see us," said Thea, "and Marjory and Monica."

"I'm sure they will," said Mary, "but I don't want you to call Mrs Clements Mammy, I don't like the name Mammy."

"Why?" The child's voice was mystified. "Why not Mammy, Aunty Mary? That is what she is called."

"I know, my darling, but she isn't your mother so it sounds rather silly. Please call her Nanny, or Granny if you like," replied Mary.

"She isn't my granny, so I can't call her that," said the child quite fiercely. "My Granny is especially special; I can't call Mammy granny."

"Well, then," said Mary, "you will have to call her Nanny." She spoke with an air of finality that brooked no argument.

Thea decided, not for the first time in her young life, that adults were stupid and unreasonable. She failed to reason out or see the need for changing a name. It was rather as if someone had suddenly said that Aunty Mary must be called Aunty Maud, or that Thea should no longer be called Thea but Dora. She decided in her mind that the safest thing was to call her nothing at all. The bus stopped frequently, by a cluster of cottages or a trackway that led up to some remote house, and people got off, mainly women laden with shopping baskets containing extra provisions for Christmas. Many looked flustered or tired, some dragging fretful youngsters with them, and some with older children who had been taken along to help carry the groceries.

At a bend in the road the bus crossed the railway line and along a lane on the left hand side was the village school. With a surge of recognition Thea pressed her face against the window and tugged at her aunt's sleeve. "Look! My school," she explained, "my school, it looks just the same."

The bus stopped to let a very large woman alight. She struggled along the gangway with bulging oilskin bags. When she was level with Thea, she looked across at her and with a beaming smile said, "Hello, luv, are yer going to see yer Mam?"

The woman obviously recognized Thea but, as she spoke, a number of people in the bus looked in her direction, causing Mary to look considerably put out. Thea smiled at the woman, although she did not know who she was. Struggling and puffing the woman heaved herself down the bus steps, standing on the grass verge looking up at the bus windows with a florid, smiling face.

"You see what I mean," said Aunty Mary. "It sounds so awful using the word Mam. Not a nice expression at all."

The bus pulled away leaving the woman standing, strangely misshapen with her heavy bags, against the dark hedgerow. Clumps of trees, farmhouses across the fields and roadside cottages became familiar to Thea and she knew that soon the wall surrounding Hacketts Cottage would appear and it would be time for them to get off the bus.

The bus came to a juddering halt and Thea made her way down the steps followed by Mary with the parcels in the basket. Standing by the old wall, everything looked familiar, for there was the sycamore tree forcing a bulge in the wall as it had done for many years, and the old steps leading up into the garden, and yet the wall had shrunk in size, seeming somehow more broken and dilapidated.

Mary caught hold of Thea's hand. "Come along, let's see how everyone is. They should have finished dinner as it's two o'clock."

They had no sooner reached the door when it was opened by Vince as he had seen them pass the window. He grinned widely at them and called, "Mam, it's Thea with a lady."

"Tell them to come in," called Mammy from the dairy, where she was washing her hands under the pump.

Thea and her aunt entered the sitting room, the sparse, untidy, rather grubby room where most of the activities of the household went on. Thea had a clear memory of the room, but in the eight months that she had been away the room had altered: it had shrunk and become more cluttered and dirty than she had remembered.

Mammy came out of the dairy and, putting her arms round Thea, kissed her, exclaiming, "My word, you have grown, at least two inches I should think." She shook hands with Mary and said, "Please take off your coats and come and sit by the fire. It is very raw today, shouldn't be surprised if we have a white Christmas."

Mary sat in a chair by the fire, while Mammy sat in the other chair and lifted Thea on to her knee. "I do believe you have got a little heavier too," she said.

The basket with the presents sat temptingly in the centre of the table, and as Vince placed their coats on the back of a chair under the window, he eyed the contents of the basket with interest. He nurtured a hope that perhaps one of the presents was for him. Monica, hearing voices, came running downstairs, then stood shyly in the centre of the room, looking at Thea almost with disbelief.

"Come along," said Mary. "Come and sit on my knee, Monica. You haven't forgotten us, have you? Surely you haven't forgotten Thea?"

Monica walked towards them. "I thought you had gone, Thea. Where had you gone?" she said, standing against Mary, who immediately lifted the little girl on to her knee.

Thea looked at Mammy's hands that held her tightly. They were such large, red, rough hands, with nails that were black and chipped, and the backs of her hands covered with veins. Her stretched out, black stockinged legs were thick and heavy, with bunions bulging through her old, black shoes. Her flowered apron was grubby, smelling of stew, onions and hen mash, and her grey hair fell in wisps round her tired wrinkled face.

Monica smiled at Thea, somewhat shyly, and said, "I'm going to school after Christmas. Are you coming to my school, Thea?"

Thea shook her head and both little girls stared at each other across the expanse of the hearth rug, while the two women chatted. Thea had looked forward so much to seeing Monica but she felt stupidly strange and tongue-tied.

The old black kettle sang on the hob and the soot burnt in a hundred little stars at the back of the grate. Marjory used to tell them that they were armies fighting and they used to guess which side would win. Thea hadn't thought about the armies in the grate since she last looked into the old fireplace eight months or so previously. "Look, Monica, look at the soldiers," she said. "I think the soldiers on your side are winning."

Both little girls leaned towards the fire–guard, their faces lit by the glow from the burning coals. Vince moved over and sat against the guard drawn by the warmth of the chatter and said, "You coming back, Thea?"

Thea shook her head. "I'm with Aunty Mary," she said.

Vincent's jersey had holes in both sleeves, the pockets of his trousers were ripped, and his boots worn and cracked across one sole. His knees and hands were chapped and there was a sore on his neck where the edge of the jumper rubbed. Although the firelight made his freckles stand out and the red lights in his hair shine, he looked pale and under the weather, seeming pleased to sit by the fire.

"I'm finding it hard going," said Mammy. "Looking after the children and working at the farm is almost too much these days. I suppose it is because I'm getting older." She rubbed her bristly chin with her hand and went on, "They asked me a few weeks ago to have two little girls, sisters, whose mother had died, and the father couldn't cope. They are decent kids but they are miserable and unhappy. I think the mother made a lot of them and now they feel adrift, but here they have to be one of the family. I can't give them individual attention."

"It's hard on youngsters when that sort of tragedy strikes," said Mary sadly. "Very, very hard."

"Marjory will be back in shortly with them," said Mammy. "She is very good, in fact I don't know what I would do without her. They want her to stay on at school." Mammy leaned forwards and her voice trembled with pride. "I have to discuss it with the authorities. It depends on a lot of things, in particular her grandmother."

"I didn't realize," said Mary, "but why her grandmother?"

"She is her legal guardian. She has ideas about Marjory leaving school, getting a job and going to live with her, so keeping her in her old age. Terrible sauce, I think it is," said Mammy with force, "especially as she has never bothered with the girl."

The dairy door opened suddenly and a draught of cold air swept through the sitting room. Marjory called, "It's ever so cold, Mam, I think it's going to snow."

"Come on in," called Mammy, "bring the girls in and we'll have a cup of tea." She got up from her chair, putting Thea into the seat she had just vacated. The cushion was warm, so Thea snuggled back into the chair and watched Mammy arranging the black kettle on to the coals. The kettle, not being far from boiling, began to sing.

Rubbing her hands from the cold, Marjory entered the sitting room followed by girls of around eight to nine years of age. They sat on the black horse hair sofa by the window while Marjory went towards the fire to warm herself. In spite of her red nose and slight blueness to her cheeks from the cold, she was developing into a striking girl, for she had beautiful eyes, a fine bone structure and marvellously clear skin.

She bent towards Thea to kiss her. "How's my little Thea?" she said. She smelt of cold and woodland and so had a delightful, frosty freshness about her person. She smiled at Mary and said, "I expect the bus was packed with Christmas shoppers." She sat on the guard, putting her foot out on the side of the chair where Thea was sitting. It was noticeable that her lisle stockings were greatly mended and her shoes very much worn at the heel.

A great surge of love for Marjory flowed through Thea's body, for she was suddenly strikingly aware of the inequalities of life. Here was beautiful, gentle Marjory with patched stockings and an old skirt, while people like Angela and Stella had everything in the world they could wish for, but were nowhere nearly as pretty and as good as Marjory.

She knew she didn't want to live with them at Hacketts Cottage ever again, because she liked the clean calmness of her aunt's house, but she wished so much that Marjory could have some nice clothes to wear.

Marjory, looking very intently at Thea, at her nicely made dress, neat stockings and polished shoes, said, "I don't expect you would want to come back here?"

For a few seconds Thea didn't know what to say, for however she answered she would hurt someone's feelings.

Mary stepped in and said, "Thea was very happy here, she loved you all, but she is my little girl now."

Thea knew in her heart that she wasn't happy at Hacketts Cottage because of all the endless chaos and shouting. Apart from Marjory, no one ever had time to talk or be gentle. Not for anything in the world would Thea change her life voluntarily, as she loved being with her aunt. She had accepted her life as it was and counted as normal the fights between the antagonistic adults and the general turmoil of the cottage.

Having been away, however, she realized that peace and order were much more to her liking, for it wasn't the normal thing for adults to be constantly at each other's throats. Robert and Mary never raised voices to each other in her presence and tried very hard to maintain marital harmony.

Mary turned to the two little girls who were sitting quietly on the sofa and said, "Tell me, what are your names?"

They sat as close as possible to each other, as if to present a single unit. The older one replied shyly, "We are Ivy and Rose." They both kept their eyes downcast, seeming terrified of being involved in any conversation.

"We have all been for a walk in the wood," volunteered Marjory, "and we have collected beech nuts, sweet chestnuts and a big sackful of wood from under the trees for kindling the fire."

Mammy cleared the big scrubbed table in the centre of the room, by placing the basket with the presents on to the sideboard and throwing the newspapers and other odds and ends on to the window-sill. She placed cups and saucers on the table, together with a large home-made fruit cake and a plate of thickly cut bread and butter.

"We'll wait for Tom and Laurie," explained Mammy. "They won't be long as they haven't been into town, but have been giving a hand on the farm."

No amount of persuading would encourage the little girls to move from the sofa or engage in conversation. It was only after Tom and Laurie had arrived that Mammy called everyone round the tea that they moved, taking their places at the table.

Laurence, extrovert and forceful, dominated the conversation, while Tom a hunched up and wizened figure, made grunting sounds of approval or disapproval while munching the bread and butter with his rubbery gums. He kept his cap on and made slurping noises while he drank his tea. Mammy shot looks of disgust in his direction, but he appeared not to notice and just went on eating.

"I told the Tarrents," exclaimed Laurie, "that quite a number of those ewes will lamb in the next week or so, and that if the weather is going to be bad they ought to be brought into the big barn. We don't want lambs born on ground covered in snow."

"Do you think it will snow then for Christmas?" enquired Mary. "I hope not. I don't like snow at Christmas."

Thea looked around the room and realized that there was nothing in the house that would suggest that Christmas was near. There was no tree, or decorations, or cards, in fact looking around the room it could be any time of the year, apart from the pile of parcels that they had brought. Laurie gave Mary a pitying glance, as though to say how out of touch some people were with matters of the countryside. "It hardly matters whether it is Christmas or not when it snows, but it's not good at any time to leave lambing ewes out in the snow. Much better to keep them dry and to keep your eye on them," he said.

Mary sensed that Laurie thought Christmas celebrations a little trivial, so she said, somewhat timidly, "Are you going to be farmer?"

Laurie, his mouth somewhat full of fruit cake, looked at her with clear blue eyes and in a very direct way answered, "No, I'm not, I'm going to study medicine. I hope to be a surgeon and specialize in some aspect of surgery that interests me."

Tom paused for a moment in his munching and, giving a toothy grin, said, "He'll be cutting us all up one of these days, then he'll be happy."

Thea didn't know what a surgeon was, or what the work entailed, but when Tom said 'cutting us all up' she thought of Jenny and it made her shiver. She couldn't think of anything worse than cutting people up.

It was dark when Thea and Mary walked across the lane to catch the five o'clock bus into Worcester. Goodbyes had been said and the gifts had been left on the dresser to be opened on Christmas morning. Thea would have loved to have seen everyone unwrapping their gifts to see if they were pleased, but Aunty Mary had suggested that Christmas morning was the time to undo gifts. Mammy had pulled a hat on her head, put on her thick, old coat and accompanied them to the bus stop.

The sky was sparkling with stars and Mammy said that it didn't smell of snow, so she was sure that they would have no difficulty getting home. She carried a hurricane lamp to light them along the garden path and down the lane to the bus stop. Thea stood in the circle of flickering light in her cherry coloured coat, with its red velvet collar and pockets.

Mammy looked at her long and hard and had quite a wistful tone in her voice when she said, "You wouldn't want to come back to your old Mammy now, would you?"

Thea looked up at her, noticing in the soft light from the lantern how old and sad she looked. Her features seemed far less severe than usual, but each wrinkle reflected intensity of feeling. "Aunty Mary would be lonely if I came back to you," said Thea. She kept her eyes on the older woman's face so that she could see what reaction her words would have, because, as young as she was, she was aware how easily people could be hurt.

Mammy smiled, a weary, resigned sort of smile, and, putting her hand on Thea's head, said, "Of course, love, you are all your Aunty has got. You must be a good girl and make her happy." Mammy looked so forlorn and tired and, because of the cold, was hunched up into her coat collar.

"Thea is going to call you Nanny," said Mary. Her voice sounded brittle so that the older woman seemed almost to wince at her words.

"Whatever you think best," she replied quietly. At that moment the bus came round the bend of the road, so she bent down and kissed Thea, brushing the child's cheek with her bristly chin.

"Goodbye, Mammy, have a nice Christmas," said Thea, being well aware that she would possibly upset her aunt, but she suddenly felt very sorry for her older foster mother.

Climbing up the bus steps, Thea stood in the gangway and waved through the bus window at Mammy standing, a dark shadow with just her face illuminated by the light from the bus head lamps.

"Well, that's that episode over," said Mary with relief in her voice, as she eased herself into the bus seat, placing the empty shopping basket on her knees. Thea slid into the seat by the side of her, feeling a little cross that Aunty Mary should have called the visit an 'episode'. For a few minutes they rumbled along in silence, both wrapped up in their own thoughts as they watched the conductor who was whistling as he looked out into the darkness.

"Mrs Clements ought not to work so hard," said Mary suddenly. "She deserves a rest, poor thing. I don't know how she manages. The silly thing is she has allowed herself to be talked into taking two other children. A big mistake, I think, and I'm sure Uncle Robert would agree."

Thea nodded, but she didn't know what to say, so she snuggled up close to her aunt and the comforting fur of her coat collar and went to sleep.

Chapter Six

FOR the first six years of Thea's life, she had been part of a gaggle of children, but since living with her aunt and uncle she had been the only child, and although wallowing in the luxury of individual attention, there were times when she longed for a companion in the house, particularly when the cold, dark evenings made playing out of doors an impossibility.

"Couldn't Marjory and Monica come?" she asked, but that suggestion was brushed aside as being impractical. She would have liked Gloria and Isabelle to have stayed but she knew that even the mention of them was taboo since the afternoon of Isabelle's birthday, when she had told her aunt about the sharp words spoken between Stella and Isabelle's mother. She wished that she hadn't mentioned the incident—but she had, so there was nothing she could do about it. Adults could be very stubborn and unreasonable.

"Have I no cousins?" she asked. "Everyone except me has cousins."

"I have a cousin," said Mary, "and he has a little boy and girl. I haven't seen them for ages, but perhaps we'll invite them after Christmas, and see if the little girl Loretta would like to stay."

"So I have got cousins," exclaimed Thea excitedly. "Ask them, go on, ask them."

"They are your second or third cousins—but still cousins," replied Mary. "The little girl is a couple of years younger than you, but you could take care of her, and be a big sister to her. I'll write to them. They are your Great Aunt Lucy's grandchildren."

Thea pictured an enormous aunt, twice the size of Aunty Margaret, with a large hat sitting on top of a pile of grey hair. "Is she very great?" she asked.

Aunty Mary looked surprised and said, "No, only one great, not great great."

In fact Aunt Lucy came for Christmas, and much to Thea's surprise was quite ordinary, and not much bigger than Granny. She stayed with Granny and Aunty Margaret, and they had dinner on Christmas Day with Robert and Mary.

Mabel arrived at the Cottage on Christmas Eve in a flurry of furs and presents. She talked of the crowded streets in the centre of Birmingham, and how lovely the decorated shops looked. Her general air of agitation and longing suggested that she wouldn't be staying long, and that she had arrived to spend the festive season with her family more out of duty than desire.

The cousins arrived as arranged on the day after Boxing Day, just after Mabel had returned to Birmingham. The children, aged three and four, were thin children with fair hair and blue eyes. The little boy, Colin, seemed reluctant to move away from his mother, but the girl was more self-assured. However, when her parents got back into the car after tea ready for the homeward journey, she looked very crestfallen as she waved them goodbye. Mary cuddled her and even her grandmother was moved to compassion, fetching her box of necklaces and allowing the child to play with them.

The little girls got on well, but with the two-year age gap they often played separately although content to be in each other's company. Thea however felt a nagging jealousy inside her when she saw her aunt cuddling and fondling the younger child. She liked Loretta, but she wanted to be first in her aunt's affections, feeling very threatened when her love was divided.

Her jealous feelings were brought to a head one evening at bath time. The girls were playing in the bath and Mary was soaping them all over with her big bath sponge rich with sweet smelling sandalwood soap. They were laughing together happily but, when it came to getting out of the bath, Mary lifted Loretta out, wrapping her in the big white bath sheet with the pink stripe at the end, and carried her into the bedroom by the fire to dry. Mary had always wrapped Thea in the bath sheet, taking her by the fire in her bedroom to dry, so the child couldn't believe that her aunt's affections could be transferred so easily.

"Are you going to fetch me, Aunty?" she called, suddenly filled with dismay at her rejection.

"You're a big girl," came the reply. "Wrap yourself in a towel and come along into the bedroom."

"I can't," shouted Thea, her eyes filling with tears.

"Of course you can," called her aunt. "A big girl like you can get out of the bath on her own!"

Thea didn't feel a big girl and for a few moments she hated her cousin more than anything else in the world. She could hear her aunty playing with the little girl's toes and the silver giggling echoed out of the bedroom, so she decided that she would stay in the bath until the water was icy cold and she frozen in the water, then perhaps her aunty would care. She twirled the soapy water round miserably, squeezing the sponge between her hands and watching the water cascade over her knees. After a few minutes she began to feel chilled and, although she didn't want to, she decided that the best policy was to get out of the water, put an alien towel round her and join her aunt and her cousin in the bedroom. When she entered the room, Loretta was already in her nightdress and Aunty Mary was brushing her hair. Thea stood miserably in the doorway and shivered.

"Come along," said Mary, as though nothing was any different. "Come and finish drying by the fire."

Thea sat down on the rug, but the warmth of the fire couldn't melt the icy, black lump that sat in her heart.

The next morning she asked if she could take her cousin to play in the almshouse garden. Mary looked thoughtful and very carefully considered the situation. "She is very young. I'm not sure whether she should be allowed out of the garden. I'm not sure whether her mother would allow it."

"I'll take care of her," said Thea. "We will just go and play in the garden—we won't hurt."

"All right," agreed Mary, "but you hold her hand very tightly and make sure that you take care of her. You must be like her big sister and not allow her to do anything silly."

Wrapped warmly in thick coats, woolly hats and gloves, and stout wellingtons, the little girls set off across the common and along the avenue of limes towards the church. The mildness of the Christmas period had gone, being replaced by a thin wind which cut across from the hills. Its sharpness was deceived by intermittent sunlight which, when it shone, was unseasonably bright. The almshouse gardens were quiet and uninteresting as there were no old people about, no cats, no gardeners, for the keenness of the wind had cloistered them indoors.

"Let's go down across the fields to the woods and the brook," said Thea, suddenly exhilarated at having someone to show off her secret haunts to. She grabbed her young cousin's hand and ran off through the gate at the end of the garden and down across the meadow towards the woods. Loretta stumbled several times in her struggle to keep up with the pace of her cousin and by the time they reached the woods her cheeks were flushed and she was panting with the effort. Rooks, sitting in groups on the naked branches of the trees, squawked hoarsely to each other while the odd wood pigeon flapped noisily across the undergrowth beneath the trees. Apart from that there was a strange silence in the woods with no other birds or wildlife visible.

"I don't like it here," said Loretta. "Let's go home."

"I'll show you the stream," replied Thea. "Come and see the stream where I catch minnows." She caught hold of her cousin's hand and began to run through the trees. The fallen wood cracked under their wellingtons as they ran and they stirred up the rank smell of toadstools and leaf mould.

"There's the brook," said Thea, standing on the steep bank of a fast flowing stream. "That's where I catch minnows."

Minnows didn't mean a thing to Loretta, so she stood there looking down into the water with a complete lack of interest. "I would still rather go home," she announced.

The stream flowed clear and cold, curling over tree roots washed and grey like the twisted limbs of very ancient men. Thin sunlight slanted through the trees, throwing curious spotted lights on to the water.

"I've caught minnows in a jam pot," expounded Thea with pride in her voice. "I'll see if I can get one now."

She slithered down the bank of the stream, clinging on to an overhanging branch to prevent her slipping into the water. "They are difficult to see," she called to her cousin, who was standing on the bank seeming almost lost in her woolly hat and wellingtons. "Come down here and see if you can see one." She held out her hand to the smaller girl.

Rather gingerly, Loretta put her wellington down on the bank and leant down to take Thea's hand, but as she did so her feet slipped from under her and she slid down the mud landing in the brook. As the cold water filled her wellington boots she let out a loud scream which set the rooks off in a chorus of raucous cawing. Thea grabbed her and pulled her out of the water and started to drag her up the bank, but the child was so frightened that she could do little to help herself, so she fell over again dragging Thea with her.

Thea thrashed around on the slippery bank, trying desperately to get the smaller child on to the edge, away from the dangerous water, but she herself had little strength and the struggle was enormous. Eventually, however, she managed to get anchorage from an overhanging branch by placing her feet firmly into the step of a root. With great effort she dragged the little girl free only to slip again and land herself headlong in the water, pushing the smaller child in front of her. For a few seconds she lay on the bottom of the stream with the icy water lapping over her face and neck. She struggled to get up but the weight of her water–logged coat pulled her down again.

She could hear Loretta screaming and lashing around in the water, but she was so choked with water, so stupefied with the coldness and terror of the situation that she couldn't find a voice. Suddenly the force of the water pushed her little cousin against her but as the child grabbed out for anchorage she prevented Thea from lifting her face from the water. She lay with Loretta clinging to her neck screaming in sightless terror, while she struggled heroically to free her mouth and nose from the water.

Suddenly from nowhere a large wellington boot materialised in front of her eyes and a strong arm lifted her up and flung her on to the bank. As Thea gasped for breath her petrified cousin was flung beside her. The man tall, dark, fierce, with a gun under his arm climbed up the bank, and looked down at them.

"Where do you live?" he demanded to know.

Thea began to cry. "By the farm. Opposite the farm," she sobbed.

"Pretty kettle of fish to be drowning yourselves," he said, picking up Loretta and sticking her under his arm. He held out his hand to Thea. "Come on you silly young wench, I'll take you home."

Loretta continued to scream and Thea squelched along miserably sobbing quietly to herself. Because her boots were water laden progress was slow, so after a few minutes the man picked her up too so that he could move quickly to unload the sopping packages that he had rescued.

Mary seeing him coming along the pathway opened the door quickly and blanched at the spectacle that confronted her.

"Here you are Missus—they were nearly gonners I can tell you. Good job I was in the wood, pigeon shooting."

Mary screamed out with disbelief. "My God, my God! What were you doing?"

Thea, now safely home, screamed loudly and Loretta joined her in with vigour. "I slipped," yelled Thea, "and she slipped too."

Mary bundled them into the kitchen almost beside herself with emotion and disbelief, while the rescuer leant on the door post, his gun slung across his shoulder, a quiet satisfied smile on his face. She began to pull the soaked clothes off the girls, tears streaming down her face as she did so.

"I'm much obliged to you," she called. "You must let me have your name and address. I must thank you later when I've calmed the girls."

"That's all right Missus, think nothing of it. It was a good job I was there," he said shutting the door and walking briskly up the path.

Mary wrapped the children in rugs and sat them by the fire. Once the shock and fear had subsided a little, she began to get cross with Thea.

"You're a naughty, naughty girl," she said. "You were nearly drowned and so was the baby."

"It was her fault," sobbed Thea defensively. "She slipped on the bank and I tried to get her back."

"You shouldn't have been by the brook—in fact you shouldn't have been in the wood. You are a naughty, naughty girl. You must not go out of the garden again ever, ever," Mary said, her voice brittle with emotion. She picked Loretta up from in front of the fire and held her close to her. The child now over her terror stopped crying, but great sobs still shook her body.

Thea clung to the fireguard her fingers intertwined through the protective meshing. She couldn't believe her aunt's anger, and was unable to comprehend her fear. All she saw was her cousin being cuddled, her aunt's tear stained angry face and she herself, rejected from all love because she had fallen in the brook. The heat of the fire was hot against her face but she couldn't move away, instead she leant her forehead on the bars and howled.

"You mustn't tell anyone," commanded Mary. "You mustn't say I allowed you out of the garden."

Thea looked up. "Why?" she asked.

"Because I shall get the blame. What do you think Loretta's mother would say or Granny? They would never forgive me."

"How's it your fault? You said it was my fault." Thea demanded to know.

"You are not to say anything. You mustn't talk about it. Your coats will have to be cleaned and I just hope they are cleanable."

Thea's tears continued to cascade down her cheeks and her nose was running horribly. She didn't care about the coat, she hoped it was ruined, then she would never have to wear it again. She pictured it sitting in the middle of the kitchen floor like a pathetic, drowned animal. Mary began to gather herself together, to clear her wits from the awful shock.

If that fierce-looking man, who looked like a gypsy poacher hadn't been there, the girls would have been drowned, and she would have had all the condemnation of the family and neighbourhood piled on her head for allowing them to wander off. They would say she wasn't a suitable person to have charge of children. She shuddered at the prospect of what might have happened.

"I'll bath you both and clear up the mess before Uncle Robert comes home," she said. "I don't want you to say anything to him either."

Thea was astounded. "Mustn't we tell Uncle Robert?"

Guilt swept over Mary for she hated lies. "Well, you can say you slipped in the water, but there is no need to say the man rescued you."

"But if he hadn't we would still be in the brook."

"I know, but there is no need to worry him by going into details, you know how he worries. It would be wrong to upset him, just say you slipped, and leave it at that." Mary knew as she issued instructions that she wouldn't get away with it, for Robert would probe and enquire until he had the truth. Getting up and placing the smaller child wrapped in a rug in the chair, she went into the kitchen to clear up the mess.

It was worse than she had imagined for water from the wellington boots lay in threatening puddles over the tiled floor, with the clothes gaumed in a red slimy mud sitting like islands in their midst. With undignified haste she scooped up the wellingtons and coats, put them outside, then gathered up the rest of the garments and hid them in the washing boiler, before she mopped the water from the floor. She must be quick for she didn't want Robert to see the devastation and if her luck held out she would have the children bathed and freshly dressed before he arrived back.

It was in the spring that Thea first noticed a change in Uncle Robert. It was difficult for her to define the change, but he seemed more preoccupied and distant, and disinclined to play games with her. He was never unkind and always answered gently when she asked him anything, but he rarely began a conversation with her, and showed little real interest in what she was doing.

Aunty Mary remained unaltered, except that when the first warm days of summer began, Thea noticed that she was always resting on her bed and seemed disinclined to go for walks. She would often sit in the shade under the apple trees, looking very contented and inactive. Then Thea noticed that she seemed to dislike housework; in fact a woman came in to clean and polish, while Aunty Mary did very little.

One beautiful early summer afternoon, when the garden was flamboyant with roses, Evelyn Booth came to tea, and the meal was served out of doors. The women sat and chatted while Thea leaned against a tree reading, with her sandwiches on a plate on her knees. Being able to read and eat was a luxury that was allowed in the garden when the atmosphere was free and relaxed.

"Listen to what it says in this story," exclaimed Thea with excitement in her voice. "If you find a dappled apple lying in the grass under an apple tree, it means someone is going to have a baby."

The two women suddenly burst out laughing and found the story very amusing, much to Thea's surprise. "A dappled apple, well I never," laughed Evelyn. "Mary," she tapped her friend's arm, "When did you find a dappled apple?"

Thea looked up and said, "Well, do you know someone who is going to have a baby then?"

Mary was laughing, but noticing the child's puzzled face said, "I am, darling."

It took several seconds for the enormity of the information to sink into Thea's understanding, and when it did, she spluttered with disbelief. "You are, Aunty Mary, you, going to have a baby?"

"Not for a long time yet, dearest, not until the autumn," Mary replied. "I hope you will be pleased to have a baby in the house."

"Oh yes, it will be lovely," replied Thea, "really lovely."

"I want you to be happy about it. I don't want you to be jealous. There will be no need for you to be jealous, as you are so much older," said Mary. "You really will be a big sister."

Thea sat against the tree with the book opened on her lap, thinking about the situation. She had never thought very seriously about babies, and it had certainly never entered her head that Aunty Mary would have children of her own. The idea of the baby was certainly pleasant; it would be lovely to be able to look after a baby. She realised why Aunty Mary was resting, as the growing baby would make her tired.

Aunty Mary's voice cut into her thoughts. "I shall have to teach you how to knit so that you can make mittens and bootees for the baby."

Thea looked up and smiled at her aunt and said "Yes, I would like that," and then went back to her day-dreaming about the infant.

When Thea saw her Granny the next day, she wanted to talk about the baby. Granny explained to her that Aunty Mary must rest as she was not a young girl, so there were bound to be difficulties at her age.

"Aunty Mary isn't old," said Thea.

"She is forty," replied Granny, "and forty is not a good age to have a baby. She must have lots of rest, so you must be a good girl and help her."

Thea had thought little about age, but forty certainly sounded old; in fact it sounded very old.

"Is Uncle Robert forty too?" enquired Thea.

"Your uncle is forty-five," expounded Granny. "They are not a young couple, so it is not going to be easy for them."

The tone of Granny's voice suggested that she thought it quite a miracle that they were having a baby at all, but Thea couldn't tell whether her attitude was one of disapproval or foreboding.

That summer Thea spent several days on her own with her grandmother, happy, sun-kissed days with Granny exclusively to herself. They spent a lot of time walking on the hills and strolling through the woods.

The hills, gentle, round and maternal, never tired the small girl or her grandmother. Together they roamed the ridges and the valleys. They felt a marvellous freedom walking over the soft, thyme-scented, sun-dried grass and watching the harebells and quaker grasses tremble in the ever present west wind which swept across the quiet Herefordshire countryside from the wild Welsh mountains. They enjoyed watching the wind bending the sorrel until it flowed like russet-coloured water across the hills and buffeting the meadow pipits who, in attempting to rise from the grass, were pushed horizontally along.

Thea had pointed out to her places of interest in the valleys, which on the eastern side lay like a giant, brilliantly coloured patchwork quilt and, on the west, like a snug, woolly rug knitted in shades of green. Thea picked the wild flowers and her grandmother identified them for her, showing her how to press them, so that their beauty and freshness would remain to be looked at during the dark days of winter.

One day, sitting under the shade of a sycamore tree at the top of a very steep valley which ran directly up from the little town, the older lady turned to the child and said gently, "Can you not feel the presence of God everywhere on these hills?"

Thea looked puzzled, not understanding what her grandmother meant, for to her God was only associated with the church, so she said, "God is in heaven and in the church."

"No, my darling," came the reply. "God has very little to do with the actual building called a church, but He is a spiritual being encompassed in all life, so His spirit is to be found on hills, in flowers, in the fields, and even," she added sadly, "in slums and among great hardship and suffering."

Thea didn't understand what her grandmother meant, so she gazed down the valley which seemed as still as a painting and across at the opposite sun-baked hill, wondering how God could be everywhere. To her, God sat comfortably in a chair in Heaven, which was a safe distance away, above and beyond the clouds. She would much rather God stayed there than wandered around with them on the hills. She realised that He did visit the church as, after all, that was His house, but He didn't interfere, He just sang and floated back to heaven smelling nicely of incense.

Thea's grandmother leaned back against the tree, and with a far-away look in her blue eyes, said, "God isn't a person you know, He is the embodiment of love in the world, and love, my darling, is unselfishness."

"Is He?" exclaimed Thea. "Then why do you call Him 'He' if He is not a person?"

The older lady smiled and said, "It is difficult to explain, but all we must do is love one another, be unselfish, and to forgive anybody we feel has wronged us." She patted Thea's knee tenderly and added, "You go on being a good girl, go to church and enjoy the services, and you will grow to understand what I mean."

Towards the end of August Thea went to stay with Great Aunt Lucy who was Loretta's grandmother. Mary felt that the child needed a bit of variety before going back to school as she was conscious of the fact that her pregnancy was rather dominating family life, so she decided a few days away for Thea would be a good idea.

Great Aunt Lucy lived in decaying splendour but her house and garden were a paradise of large rooms full of endless muddle and an overgrown garden which resembled a northern jungle.

Once objects got put in a certain place, there they remained, accumulating dust and making a haven for spiders. Objects belonging to her late husband and parents cluttered cupboards and table tops. The walls were covered with dusty pictures and there were pieces of porcelain whose beauty and colour were quite obscured.

One of the most exciting places in the house was the attic. This consisted of three large rooms, which during the more affluent years of the house had been the servants' bedrooms. Anything not required was not thrown away, but merely placed in the attic with the other forgotten objects, until the floors literally groaned under the weight. To a child the wealth of interest was immeasurable, being akin to Aladdin's cave.

The front garden was kept tidy, and a lawn to the side of the house was neatly trimmed so that Great Aunt Lucy could sit out under the trees when the weather was warm enough. The rest of the garden grew in wild exuberance, with trees, bushes and flowering shrubs of the most exotic varieties jostling for ground space with the humble briars and crawling honeysuckle. Birds built their nests among the green confusion, and a fox had an earth under one of the rotting sheds. Altogether it was a garden where wild things seemed to live in natural harmony, and where children could become part of their existence.

Great Aunt Lucy kept one small sitting room and her own bedroom reasonably habitable, but she had little interest in what happened to the rest of the house, so generations of mice bred unchecked and moths lived in their private galaxy of old blankets. She herself was far from senile, for she had a mind that was active and very interested in the world around her; it was just that she felt housework far beneath her and couldn't get herself motivated towards rubbish clearance.

When Thea played in the attic, her aunt would sometimes climb the stairs and poke around among the trunks and old chests of drawers. One day Thea lifted the lid of a rusty tin trunk and found inside a Victorian wedding dress of cream brocaded silk. It was wrapped in sheets of old newspapers, then tied up in a large linen sheet, but when the parcel was undone the dress was dust-free and as fresh and beautiful as the day when it had been worn.

Great Aunt Lucy fingered the dress almost sadly. She explained how the dress had been her mother's wedding dress, having been placed in the trunk for her to wear when she became a bride.

"Things didn't turn out as my mother would have wished," she said. "She would have liked me to have married, as a young woman, some handsome wealthy gentleman, but I disappointed her."

"Do you think anyone will ever wear it now?" asked Thea.

"Doubt it," replied Aunt Lucy. "Let us wrap it up again carefully and put it away in the trunk." Sitting there in the musty confusion of the attic, Aunt Lucy enraptured her niece by telling her about the family and about her childhood. The family on her father's side could trace their ancestry back hundreds of years. "The family seems to have put a curse upon it," said Aunt Lucy, brushing the dust from her navy-blue silk dress; then lowering her voice in a conspiratorial manner, she leaned towards Thea and added, "It was a gypsy that did it, you know."

"A gypsy put a curse on the family? How?" gasped Thea, feeling a shiver of fear and excitement run down her spine.

"It's best not to talk about it too much," explained Aunt Lucy, "but it was apparently my grandfather that caused it. He had some sort of association with a gypsy girl who put a curse on him, and said that the family would die out, but before it did there would be no love or happiness in their marriages."

"Can gypsies put curses on people?" enquired the child.

Aunt Lucy laughed. "I don't know," she said, "but it's best not to cross gypsies. I believe in playing safe and not upsetting them."

"Do you really think the family will die out?" asked Thea. "Really die out and be no one left?"

Aunt Lucy explained that the words 'dying out' didn't mean that no one remained, but it meant that there were no boys to carry on the family name, so in effect the family died out.

In the garden Thea built a secret den, where she would hide while the hot August sun threw striped shadows through the vegetation and the fox cubs chased each other round the old shed. With her teddy bear and books she was in her own special make-believe world, with no one to disturb her. Aunt Lucy, lying back in her chair under the apple tree, demanded little, so the atmosphere remained relaxed. They ate when Aunt Lucy stirred herself, otherwise they drank ginger beer and ate biscuits. Bedtime too was haphazard, but it was usually dark by the time Thea was in bed, by which time she was usually so exhausted that she fell immediately to sleep.

Aunt Lucy had ear-phones attached to her wireless so Thea loved to sit in the big armchair in the evening listening to the stories and music. It was a pleasant change, because Uncle Robert only ever listened to news on the wireless, switching the thing soundly off when the news was over. In spite of the freedom of her great aunt's house, Thea wasn't sorry to get back to the firm routine of Robert's and Mary's establishment. School and schoolfriends were greeted with relief and the rigmarole of learning tables and spellings was once again accepted as part and parcel of life.

Autumn came in with boisterous enthusiasm, scattering the leaves with high winds and driving rain. Mary rested more and more, frequently lying on the sofa looking out through the window at the storm tossed, battered garden. When Thea came home from school she would get up and prepare tea, but when Robert came home from work he would worry desperately in case she was doing too much.

Margaret came back from Bath, declaring that she had no intention of returning. She had decided to live with her mother and so be a companion for her. She had made up her mind that she would look after her sister during the period of her confinement and then get work locally. While Margaret was caring for her sister, Thea was to stay with her grandmother and so keep her company. She would very much have liked to have stayed at home and been there when the baby was born, but the grown-ups had decreed that it was better if she was away.

A nurse had been booked to live in the house during the time of the confinement and lying-in period. It had been arranged that she would sleep in Thea's room. Thea was instructed to tidy her room, taking whatever possessions she wanted to her grandmother's house.

In the cold dampness of early morning on the last Saturday in October, Thea walked with her Aunty Margaret to Granny's house. She held her teddy bear under one arm and a pile of jigsaws in a bag under the other, while Margaret carried the suitcase. She felt quiet and afraid and in a strange unexplainable way rejected. She would have liked to have stayed at home, but she knew it wasn't possible.

The nurse had arrived that morning, cool, blue and efficient, while Robert with a face like parchment had walked around in silence. Aunty Mary had stayed in her bedroom but she looked quite happy and normal when Thea had gone in to kiss her.

"Be good," she told Thea, "and when you next see me, the little stranger should be here."

On arrival at Granny's house, Margaret put the suitcase in the hall, had a few words with her mother, and then returned to her sister's house.

It seemed an endless Saturday with very little conversation and a great deal of jigsaw making. Granny, disinclined to talk or sit, had turned out drawers in an agitated, desperate manner, and had walked around the garden several times in the chilly drizzle. When it came to bedtime, Thea was allowed to choose whatever books she wanted from Granny's bookcase, so, taking advantage of Granny's mood—for usually the old lady fussed a lot about her books—she pulled out a pile of Sunday Books for Children and took them triumphantly to her bedroom.

The next morning she awoke fairly late, but the house was still and silent, so Thea took one of the Sunday Books and sat up in bed reading. The sun was shining, so the room was bright and friendly, for the gloom of the previous day had lifted. At one point she heard a car door slam, and what sounded like a back door closing; then silence again drifted into the house. A while later she heard the mouselike sounds of her grandmother moving around her bedroom, and knew then that the house was beginning to stir.

When the old lady opened the door to Thea's room she was still wearing her nightdress with her grey hair cascading down beyond her shoulders. She looked tired, but she was smiling. "A baby girl has arrived," she said gently. "A baby girl born just over an hour ago. Your aunt is all right; there were no particular problems."

Granny sat on the edge of Thea's bed, brushing her hair, then with deft experienced fingers she pulled the strands upwards, arranging them into a neat, tight bun. Thea, watching her, marvelled at how the hair responded to her touch and was transformed from the untidy mass into the neat, ordered style which seemed so much part of her grandmother. Granny's frail little form seemed almost lost in the billowing pink nightdress, with her small thin white feet sticking out from the edge looking pathetically thin.

"Dress in my room Gran, then we can talk," she said.

The old lady smiled. "If you want me to, you funny child."

"Shall I read to you while you dress," went on the child. "I'll read you the story of 'June's White Heather'."

Thea read while her grandmother put on her assortment of clothes. She hooked heavy corsets on to her thin frame, then a bodice made of pure woollen flannel, followed by two petticoats, one thick and one thin, and finally her skirt and blouse. While she was encasing herself in her armour for the day, Thea read her the story of the little girl who went in search of white heather so that she might bring luck to her family.

"Shall we go on the hills and see if we can find some white heather, Gran?" asked Thea.

Granny laughed and said, "We would have to go to Scotland, for there is only purple heather on these hills."

At the morning church service, the vicar told the congregation the good news about the baby and a special prayer was said for the family. Thea felt very important as she squeezed Granny's hand. She smiled proudly at the people who were sitting near to them, when Mary's and Robert's names were mentioned.

After dinner Thea and her Granny were like cats on hot bricks, so anxious were they for the time to pass so that they could visit Mary and the baby.

A great feeling of warmth and delight spread through Thea. She felt unbelievably happy that at last the baby had arrived.

"When can we see her?" she enquired.

"Later today," replied Granny. "We will let your aunt have a good sleep, then we will visit about tea time."

The baby lay on the bed dressed in a long white gown, and wrapped softly in a hand-crocheted shawl. She was dark-haired with a tiny exquisite face which looked up at the world in wondering puzzlement. Her small hands with their outstretched miniature fingers waved about as though grasping for some primitive anchor.

Thea was enraptured. "What are you going to call her?" she gasped.

Mary, placing her fingers lightly on the dark, downy head, said, "Joy. We shall call her Joy, for she has brought us joy beyond our wildest dreams."

"That's a nice name," said Thea. "I wonder what she will be like."

"Oh, she will be beautiful," said Mary. "She is going to have dark hair like me and lovely blue eyes like her father. Yes, she is going to be very beautiful."

"She was born on Sunday too," said Thea wistfully, "so she should be beautiful and good."

Aunty Mary smiled, a satisfied distant dreamy smile, and said "Yes, my darling, that is so. She will be good and beautiful."

Chapter Seven

WHEN Mary and Robert were struggling with their infant, Mabel unexpectedly suggested that Thea should go and stay with her in Birmingham. She didn't readily agree, but given no option, she had to resign herself to the inevitable. Mabel was her mother, she accepted that fact, but had never really thought about where Mabel lived, or what sort of work she did. However she uncomplainingly packed her suitcase and set off with Mabel on the red double-decker bus, which in itself was an exciting experience. In the centre of Birmingham, amidst the noise and confusion, Mabel hailed a taxi and they were driven several miles out of the city.

Thea, who had only ever seen the countryside, was amazed by the crowded pavements, the noise of the traffic, and the bright flashing lights which were everywhere. Mabel had come and gone with infrequent regularity in Thea's life, but the child had not considered where she had come from, or in fact where she returned to. It was therefore quite a surprise to find that she lived in a pretty, spacious flat on the first floor of a large house. The windows looked over a garden, and beyond on the skyline, were taller buildings and chimneys belching smoke.

Thea gawped around her at the elegant sitting room so devoid of any of the cosy clutter she was used to. The walls were white, the carpets and curtains a deep pink, and the upholstery white with pink flowers. The highly polished furniture looked as if fingers never touched it, and the pictures, which had been positioned to catch the light, were nearly all of nudes in various positions and postures.

"Take your coat off," instructed Mabel, "and put it in your bedroom." She nodded towards a door to the right of the hallway.

The child stood and gazed inquisitively around at the new and varied objects that were assaulting her senses, as if unable to move.

Mabel put a match to the gas fire ad switched the table lamps on. "Take your coat off you silly, you can't stand there all night."

Slowly Thea began to unbutton her coat, and then pull off the gloves and beret. As if irritated by the child's slowness Mabel grabbed the coat from her and took it into the bedroom herself. Feeling strangely denuded and isolated Thea continued to look around as if seeking something that was familiar and known. She looked at the photographs in silver frames that were grouped together on a polished table under the window and caught sight of one of herself in Mammy Clement's orchard.

"That's me," she called excitedly. "There's a picture of me."

Mabel started at the child's sudden exuberance. "That was taken the summer you started school," she said.

"I'm in the orchard with Mammy Clements," said Thea, overcoming her shyness and going over to the table. "I haven't seen Mammy Clements for a long, long time."

"She is nothing to do with us," replied Mabel in an off handed way, "so why should you see her?"

"She sent me ten shillings for my birthday."

Mabel sniffed with disapproval, and patted her hair.

"Who's this?" asked Thea, fingering a picture of a man with light hair and horn rimmed glasses.

"Come away," commanded Mabel. "You'll knock the whole lot over and break them."

"Who is it?" enquired the child.

"Oh, just a friend. Now go and hang your coat up in the wardrobe. I've put it on your bed."

Thea had only been used to hanging things up on pegs in the hall, never in wardrobes, so she was puzzled by the request.

"If you are going to stay with me you'll have to learn to be tidy. Now hang your coat up, then go and wash your hands and face."

Thea paused by the door. "Why do you live here?" she asked.

Mabel gave a small exasperated laugh. "Because I work here."

"But why don't you live with Granny?"

"What a lot of questions you ask. I live here and work here, because I want to. I have a good job which keeps me and you."

"I live with Aunty Mary," stated Thea, flabbergasted by Mabel's remarks.

"Yes but I pay for your keep. I couldn't let Aunty Mary look after you for nothing, could I?"

Thea didn't know, but she didn't like the notion of being kept. It had never entered her head that she was kept.

"It's good of Aunty Mary and Uncle Robert to look after you, but you are my daughter so I must keep you."

She walked into her bedroom, mulling Mabel's words over in her mind. 'I keep you because you are my daughter.' She was her daughter because everyone told her she was, but she knew that Mabel didn't really like her, so she didn't know how she came to be her daughter. Aunty Mary adored Joy, and told the fretful little scrap continually how much she adored her.

She hung the coat onto the strange, padded hanger and struggled to hook it on the rail in the wardrobe. She then undid her suitcase and took out Teddy and a book. She had only brought one book and she knew that wouldn't last very long, and what she would do then she didn't know. Here in Mabel's tidy flat there were no toys, puzzles or paints.

As she returned to the living room, Mabel called out, "I've got tickets for the pantomime tomorrow." She forced her voice to sound jolly as if a pantomime was the greatest of treats. "Some friends are coming and we are going to have a meal out afterwards."

Thea smiled hesitatingly, uncertain of what to expect.

"It will be fun to have supper out in the dark, won't it?"

Thea nodded, but she didn't know if it would be fun, never having done it.

"You lead such a quiet life buried away in the country."

"I like the country," said Thea defensively thinking of the commons and hills.

"One eyed place," stated Mabel contemptuously. "The life Mary and Robert lead wouldn't suit me. They are so old fashioned and parochial."

Thea was prevented from answering for at that moment the front door opened and she found herself confronted by a stranger. He was wearing a dark, heavy overcoat with a long scarf dangling from the collar and horn-rimmed glasses. His hat and gloves he held in his hand.

"Hello little one," he said with a bemused smile, as if surprised to see the child.

"Richard, darling," Mabel exclaimed, moving towards him swiftly and kissing him. "This is Thea, I've brought her back for a few days."

Thea smiled shyly, taken aback by the appearance of the stranger.

"So this is Thea?" he said. "Grown a bit since I last saw her." He took off his coat, flung it on a chair in the hall then settled himself on the settee. "Now Thea, tell me how old you are, I've forgotten."

Tongue-tied, Thea stared at him. He was the man in the photograph, but there was also something else about him which was familiar. His hair was thick and fair and curly, his blue eyes penetrating.

"Well come along. How old are you?"

"Seven. Seven and a half," whispered Thea, staring at him in amazement.

He laughed, as if amused by the child's fixed gaze. "Am I that fascinating?" he asked.

"Don't stare," commanded Mabel. "It's rude to stare. Are you staying for tea Richard?"

"Just a cup, then I must get going."

"Oh, can't you stay?"

"Just a few minutes—well, half an hour," he said glancing at his wrist watch. "I have a meeting this evening."

"You always have a meeting. I wish you'd stay."

He stretched out his hand and gave Mabel's a little squeeze. "Can't be helped, I have to earn a living. She's like you," he said, smiling at Thea.

Momentarily Mabel appeared put out. "I can't see it." She tossed her head dismissively. "I think she is like my sister."

Richard laughed again as if amused by Mabel's reaction. "She is like you—really she is. By the way do you think the kid would like to play with the gramophone?"

"She'll break it!" Mabel was astounded at his suggestion.

"Of course she won't. It might amuse her." He got up, opened a cupboard and fetched out the object.

Mabel looking very disapprovingly said, "You'll have to show her how to put the records on otherwise she'll scratch them and they will be ruined.

Richard searching for a compromise said, "The kid can turn the handle and you or I will start the record."

Thea stared at the black box that was obviously so precious to Mabel, but her amazement soon turned to delight when the music poured out. She turned the handle with enthusiasm while *Home on the Range*, *Red Sails in the Sunset*, and *When I grow to Old to Dream* filled the room. This was a toy beyond all her expectations.

All too soon Richard left and the laughter and fun left the room with him, leaving behind an empty loneliness.

"Is he your boyfriend?" Thea enquired.

"Just a friend," replied Mabel. "He has his own home and family."

"If he isn't your boyfriend, why did he kiss you?"

"Old friends always kiss," said Mabel sharply. "There isn't anything odd in giving an old friend a kiss."

"Do his wife and children come to tea?" Thea asked with innocent directness.

Mabel didn't answer, for she had gone into the kitchen with the dirty crockery. Thea was puzzled, she had never seen Aunty Mary, or Mammy Clements for that matter, fling her arms round the neck of a friend in such a way. She looked again at the photograph, even more puzzled as to why he should be on his own in a silver frame on Mabel's table. He looked so familiar, so known, but she couldn't reason why. As she gazed at the picture, she realised that the smile reminded her of Isabelle and Gloria's father.

Going to Mabel in the kitchen she asked, "Is Richard anything to do with Isabelle?"

Mabel turned, looking sharply at the child. "You are a 'nosy parker'. What makes you ask?"

"Because he looks like her."

"Yes, he's her uncle, I work for his mother, your godmother, that's how I know him."

"Has he got children?"

Mabel nodded, wiping the cups and saucers with swift agitation.

"Do they come here?"

"No! He works near here—they live a distance away. Go and play with the records if you want, but don't let the needle scratch them or they will be ruined," she said, longing for the child to do something other than ask endless questions.

Thea went into the sitting room and picked up her book. Although fascinated with the gramophone she didn't want to get the blame for scratching the records. She hoped Aunty Mary would buy one, but now they had the baby she doubted it. She went to bed without protest when Mabel suggested she did, for there was nothing for her to do. She lay with the eiderdown pulled up round her ears, listening to the mournful howling of the winter wind as it raced round the corner of the house. She wondered what Mabel was doing in the stillness of her pink and white sitting room, but no sounds penetrated the black silence of the bedroom. She seemed to have been in her dark, silent room for hours until she heard the splashing of bathwater, and with relief realized she wasn't alone.

One morning she went into the kitchen to get a glass of milk when she was confronted by Richard, perched on a stool, eating toast and reading a newspaper.

Glancing up he said, "Hello little one. Have you woken up early?"

Astounded at coming across him in the kitchen, Thea muttered, "Where's Mabel?"

"Still asleep I think," he said, taking another bite of toast, and crunching it noisily.

Thea longed to ask him how he had got in, for she hadn't heard the door bell, and anyhow why was Mabel still asleep, why wasn't she talking to her visitor? She poured out her milk and stood hesitantly by the table, wondering whether she should wake Mabel.

As if sensing the child's bewilderment, he peeped round the paper and smiled. "I'm just going to work, early meeting. Let Mabel sleep, it's a treat for her to lie in. Normally you see, at this time she should be at work."

On a late May evening, soon after the Coronation of King George VI, Robert arrived from work looking tense and pale. Flinging himself into his favourite armchair, he put his head into his hands looking a picture of abject misery. Hearing the door open and close but no voice call in welcome, Mary hurried from the kitchen where she was preparing the evening meal and stood in the doorway to the sitting room.

"What's the matter?" she enquired anxiously. "Are you ill?"

"Worse than ill," he replied, without looking up. "I'm finished."

Wiping her hands on her apron, she hurried across to him, sat on the arm of the chair and tenderly placed her arm across his shoulder. "What do you mean?" she said with tension in her voice. "How are you finished?"

Saturday's Child

He looked up at her. "I have no job. The firm has gone bankrupt."

Thea, sensing the enormity of the situation, sat silently on the sofa where she had been reading. Uncle Robert, who was always so calm and unemotional, looked as if he was about to burst into tears, so the whole situation to her was very disconcerting.

"How has this come about, Robert?" Mary asked apprehensively. "I thought the firm was sound enough. After all, you have been there for twenty years."

Robert shook his head as though recovering from a blow that had left him dazed. "Insufficient profits, lack of orders, poor management, a combination of many things."

For a few minutes they sat silently together in the chair, the only sound in the room coming from the gurgles of the baby who was lying on a rug on the floor and the grandfather clock's heavy ticking. Thea sat and looked at them, not even daring to turn a page of her book.

Mary's voice suddenly cut the silence. "You'll get another job, Robert. I'm sure you will."

"My experience is very limited and I'm on the wrong side of forty," replied Robert miserably. "Why should anyone want to employ me? The employment situation, as you know, is awful."

"I know, dear," said Mary gently, "but I am sure things will be all right. We will talk about it." She picked Joy up from her rug, taking her across to her husband. "Come and cheer Daddy up," she said.

"I had such hopes for her future," he said, kissing the soft baby arm, "but an out of work father is not going to do her much good."

"Thea, take Joy for a walk round the garden," said Mary. "Here, put her in the pram and fix the reins on, so that she won't tip over." She handed the baby to Thea. "Be a good girl and look after her for me so that I can chat to Uncle."

The baby jumped with excitement in Thea's arms, grabbing her hair with infant delight, but Thea was getting used to handling the active little bundle, so she struggled with her to the pram and started to sort out the contortion of reins.

"Thea," Mary called, "You will keep everything you have heard to yourself. Not to mention to anyone. Do you understand?"

"I shan't say anything," replied the child, although she was always puzzled why there had to be endless secrets and subterfuge. Aunty Margaret always prefixed gossip with the words, "Now you mustn't breathe a word to anyone but I must tell you . . ." Thea always felt that it was a pity when things of interest couldn't be shared around; and what's more, secrets were such terribly difficult things to keep. She remembered how several times during moments of excitement, she had let the cat out of the bag.

Thea thought that the baby would like to see the hens, so she pushed the pram into the orchard where the birds were free under the trees. The hens, thinking that food was in the offing, came running through the grass like stout old ladies and stood expectantly round the pram. Robert always shut them up in the hen house in the evening, taking food to entice them in, so they thought that a different benefactor had arrived. They looked up with quizzical eyes, making soft noises in their throats. Several scratched with their claws where the grass was thin, sending up little showers of earth, in the hope of finding some unsuspecting grub or worm.

Apart from the main hen house, there were several small pens and huts where chickens were kept, the younger ones still with the mother hens. They all had to be safely shut up at night as there were foxes around who would soon take advantage of the situation. The hens were mainly Rhode Island Reds, although there were half a dozen Black Leghorns among them. As they picked freely round the orchard, they needed very little care apart from extra corn, water and shutting up at night, but in return they produced a good quantity of eggs.

Thea sat on the trunk of an old tree which lay in the orchard, watching the hens. She wondered how long she ought to stay out with the baby, but supposed her aunt would come out and join them when she had finished discussing with Uncle. A red may tree by the orchard gate threw a heavy, pungent stale sweetness into the air, but it was hard to imagine how such tiny petals could give off such a strong scent. For a week or two in the year the grotesque twisted branches of the trees became transformed into a thing of radiant beauty and unbelievable daintiness.

The baby glanced towards Thea and rewarded her with an innocent smile of unasked for love, which stirred her emotions and for the first time made her think of her tiny cousin as a human being, something to care for, cherish and protect. She had never before been completely alone with the baby, and a great feeling of happiness and contentment flowed through her, although she felt guilty about feeling so happy, especially as the baby's father was so distraught. She knew that the baby was the most important thing in the family and precious beyond expression to her parents, so much so that Uncle Robert hadn't eyes, or time, for any other child, but somehow all that didn't matter as long as the baby loved her. One day she would grow up and be a girl and they would be great companions.

Even though Mary had reassured her husband by telling him that he would get another position, Thea wondered where it would be and if it would involve moving house. Although not yet eight years old, she had the intelligence to know that being out of work was a serious business, which could entail having to move house. She loved the house, the large informal garden with its hidden nooks, the almost wild orchard and she hoped that they would continue to live there.

The baby looked at Thea, smiling sweetly again, and Thea was suddenly filled with an unreasonable dread that she mustn't love her too much, otherwise she would be taken away from her. She thought of Jenny, how she had loved her, and the cats she had loved which had died, so deeply within her she was almost afraid to love the baby. Her awful thoughts and unreasonable fears were interrupted by Aunty Mary coming into the orchard. She looked calm, seeming quite normal and composed.

"How are my little girls?" she said. "Have you been keeping my hens company?" She sat on the seat by the side of Thea and put her arms round her shoulder. "You mustn't worry," she said. "Everything will turn out right."

Thea smiled, but she didn't like to tell her aunt that she wasn't worrying at all, in fact she was very happy.

It was a summer of turmoil and heartaches, but eventually Robert found another job. They decided to move house to save Robert having to travel to work and because they couldn't afford to stay where they were. Mary shed many tears, as she loved her old timber-framed house, but she realized that the financial situation dictated that they must find somewhere cheaper. The old house was full of romance, for she and Robert had chosen to live there when they married and it was there that Joy had been born.

The new house was a modern chalet bungalow, pebble-dashed, painted cream and situated on the outskirts of a village about three miles away, so although they were changing neighbourhoods, they remained in the locality. The new house had a fair-sized garden, a splendid view of the hills, and was altogether much easier to run than the old house.

The furniture van arrived on a warm summer's morning when the garden looked at its best. Flame-coloured poppies leant against roses and honeysuckle, and the air was heavy with their scent. The van backed into the driveway and the man got out. One of the removal men leant against the van, pushed his cap to the back of his head and gazed around with a look of wonder on his face.

"Well, ma'am," he said, "this is one of the prettiest places I've ever seen. I just can't believe anyone wanting to leave it."

Robert shot him a look of profound disapproval. "It's not from choice that we are leaving. Sometimes circumstances dictate what one has to do."

The removal man, looking slightly embarrassed, muttered, "I'm sure, Sir." As though quickly to change the subject, he added, "Just look at them poppies."

"Yes," said Mary sadly, "they are beautiful, so flamboyant, but so transient. Life is like that, snatches of beauty and then nothing."

"Let's not get morbid," said Robert. "We have work to do, so we had better get on with it."

Granny looked after Joy and Thea, while Margaret helped with the move. It was a busy, exhausting day, followed by several more, equally busy, as china had to be unpacked, curtains hung and the new house put into order. In spite of Mary's fears, the antique furniture fitted into the new house better than she could ever have imagined. In fact the bright, sunny rooms showed many of the pieces off to good advantage and Mary had to admit that, on the whole, she was very pleased.

The village they moved to was quite a lively place, containing a mixed selection of people. Children played their games on the common under the lines of flapping washing strung across from the willow trees. Years previously branches of willow had been thumped into the fertile earth as washing posts, but they had taken root and grown into sturdy trees. The tops were frequently cut to prevent the foliage getting tangled with the sheets, so they stood with heavy trunks like overweight ladies wrapped in conversation.

Artisan cottages, middle-class houses and the residences of the well-to-do looked out over the commons towards the hills, presenting a picture of a harmonious mixed community. It was in fact just the children who mixed freely, for the adults preferred to keep themselves tidily within their own confines of class, knowing their boundaries and not wishing to overstep them.

Nothing much happened in the village however that wasn't of universal knowledge. The ordinary people viewed the wealthy with interest and suspicion, lapping up any passing gossip that floated over the well tended lawns. Gardeners and housemaids had ears, although credited by their employers with having none, and the wealthy viewed the villagers with interest, noticing a great deal more than anyone would have thought possible.

Basically the people lived fairly well together, rubbing shoulders in church and at village functions. At church they met formally, each in their own seats, not by law but by force of custom. At the village fete rivalry was present in the form of the choicest blooms, largest marrows and brownest eggs, but a general friendliness prevailed over the jealousies.

Cattle and sheep, the property of the local farmers and small-holders, shared the common grass with the villagers' hens, geese and horses. There were few cars about so the animals crossed the roads unharmed, and ewes would frequently stand in the centre of the road on the warm tarmac feeding their lambs.

According to the older residents, the village was much quieter than it had been fifty years previously, when the population had been larger and a good deal wilder. True, there was the odd eccentric who cheered up the monotony of village life; otherwise the people were hardworking and thrifty, spending most of their energies earning a living and raising children.

There was a frequent bus service into the town and fast buses ran to Birmingham, Gloucester and Weston-super-Mare, so when money was available the villagers had their days out; otherwise they got on with their lives uninterrupted by the happenings of the outside world.

The children of the village played together without bothering about social status. The common and the hills were the classless neutral domains of the carefree children, who bothered little about the occupations of their parents. Instead, status was attached to those who could climb the highest trees, run the fastest and do the most daring things. As long as they kept away from their parents' gardens, few questions were asked and they were free to play together, learning a tremendous amount from each other's company.

Thea slipped happily into this society and, before starting at her new school in September, had made new friends and had taken part in exciting exploits that she would never have dreamt could have existed. She grew not only in stature but in self-confidence, and was unbelievably happy to have been accepted by the children of the village.

The grey stone church standing on the edge of the common was a humble building, giving no pretence of grandeur either in its appearance or in the manner of its divine services. From its door a most magnificent view of the hills could be seen, so the villagers surrounded by so much natural beauty used the church as a spiritual harbour rather than a springboard of inspiration.

A curate looked after the needs of the people and took the services with the help of a lay preacher, an elderly schoolmaster called Mr Hughes, who had a charismatic smile, thick white hair and a large moustache. A single bell which sounded like a galvanised bucket being struck called the faithful to worship and they came willingly, in their dozens, from the houses that stood on the edge of the common.

Sunday school, conducted by the elderly lay preacher, was held in the Institute, a short distance from the church. It was unusual for any child in the village not to attend Sunday school, as it was the normal part of the pattern of existence to gather there on Sunday afternoons. With gentle authority the unruly hordes were brought to heel by the kindly old man, who read them stories from the Bible and explained their meanings with almost theatrical eloquence, and encouraged the unmusical and tone deaf to sing lustily along with those who could do justice to an angel choir.

On hot summer days when the dusty room almost exploded with heat and straw hats stuck to sweaty heads, *In the Bleak Midwinter* would be chosen as a hymn to make the children feel cooler, and on freezing winter afternoons, when the snow was piled high against the Institute windows, *Summer Suns are Glowing* would be sung to warm them all up. Miss Gittings, the pianist, would thump out the tunes on the tinny piano and the children's shrill voices would resound across the common, much to the astonishment of people walking past.

Thea started at her new school, which was considerably larger than the old village school. There were more classrooms and more teachers. Thea had been so well-taught at the village school that she was ahead of the girls in her class in most subjects. She settled into a routine with ease and enjoyed the challenge of making new friends and adjusting to different teachers.

Although Thea was gregarious, loving the rough and tumble games with a large group of children, she developed certain friendships with children from the school which built up her self-confidence and filled a required need that strengthened her character.

With Iris, a gentle green-eyed girl, Thea developed a great attachment. Iris had no desire to compete with Thea, being content with friendship alone. She would praise and encourage, but in return would appear amazed and slightly embarrassed if compliments were thrown in her direction. She came from a secure happy home, having one older sister, a refined devoted mother, and a father who suffered from indifferent health.

Iris and Thea would share their innermost secrets during their long walks through the fields or along the soft green paths of the hills. A secret given to Iris would be perfectly safe, as torture wouldn't drag it from her. Iris's life was ordered and secure, based very much on certainties, so she was frequently amazed and puzzled by Thea's circumstances.

"Don't you know who your father is, Thea?" Iris would ask.

Thea would shrug her shoulders in what appeared to be disinterest and say "What does it matter?"

One day when they were sitting in the tall grasses on the edge of the cornfield, Iris said, "Aren't you curious about your father? Don't you want to meet him and know all about him?"

Thea, looking unabashed, lying on her back sucking the end of a piece of grass, said, "It's no interest to me, I don't care. What difference does it make, anyway?"

"No interest?" Iris was astounded. "I would be interested to know who my father was."

"Only because you know who he is," said Thea laughingly, "and that makes you think that it is important."

The corn threw shadows of dark gold, like the stripes on tigers, across the faces of the girls. The grass, the poppies and the hot summer sunshine cocooned them in an oasis of confidences.

"I like your mother," confided Iris. "I think she is ever so modern."

Thea, glancing at her friend with amusement and surprise, said, "You don't really know my mother. The awful thing about my mother is that she flirts."

Iris, flicking the powdery seeds from the top of a head of grass, said seriously, "Why do you think she does that, Thea?"

Thea shrugged her shoulders. "She likes to be noticed, I suppose. She wants people to like her, especially men. I hate it when she flirts. I am never going to flirt!" She said the last statement with firm resolution.

"How do you know what you are going to do?" said Iris, throwing a lump of grass at her friend.

"Because," said Thea, "I shall never marry!"

"Oh, Thea!" exclaimed Iris. "Surely you'll marry. I shall marry and have four children. They will be beautiful children."

"Thea, you are such a lovely person, I know you will get married," soothed Iris, trying to placate her friend. "Your children will be marvellous."

Thea lay on her stomach looking through the wild poppies towards her friend's innocent face. "I shall be a very clever doctor," she said.

Iris, looking up, replied, "I'm sure you will, Thea, if you want to be. I want a handsome husband, a lovely house and four children. If you want to be a doctor, I am sure that is just as wonderful."

It was with Iris that Thea would watch the kingfisher fishing over the stream that ran through the wood, pick cowslips and hunt for the rare wild orchids, but Mavis, on the other hand, was quite a different friend. Mavis had fair hair, serious dark eyes and a friendly open face. Her background was very similar to Thea's for she was living with her aunt, while her mother and stepfather lived on the south coast. Mavis loved her aunt and older cousin, but she nursed a resentment towards her mother, basically because she had chosen to marry and so reject her daughter.

Thea and Mavis used to read poetry together, discuss the books they had read and plan their futures. These were secret discussions and they let no one else share their secrets, apart from Iris who was allowed to look at the secret code. Having drawn her into their confidence, they were somewhat shattered when her older sister found a secret letter and cracked the code with relative ease.

Mavis, like Thea, loved school, but she showed a particular interest in science, planning one day to be a scientist who would discover something of world-shattering importance.

"There is so much suffering in the world, and so much that needs to be discovered," Mavis would say, "and I am going to play a part."

Thea, looking at her friend, knew that whatever she set out to achieve she would accomplish. She felt that too about Dorothy, who lived with her parents and brothers in a small house by the pub. She was a beautiful Aphrodite of a girl, with long golden hair and eyes the colour of flax. Anything in life she wanted she would get because she was beautiful, and Thea envied her.

Chapter Eight

MARY and Robert settled down well in the village and made many new and quite unexpected friends. Although Mary in many ways pined for her lovely half-timbered house, she was of such a nature that she looked for the best in what she had, and in a short while began to love her modern little house and decided that it was much easier to keep in order.

The village was so situated that long, interesting walks could be undertaken with little effort. Often on Saturdays when Robert was busy or sleeping through exhaustion because of his work during the week, Mary would pack a picnic, put it in the pram, and she and Thea would go walking and visiting. They would walk across the common and the golf course and head towards the southern end of the hills.

One elderly lady that they visited was in her late nineties, but in her day she had been a champion of women's liberation. She lived in a pretty cottage looking up towards the hills and was looked after by her nurse companion. She had been a headmistress so retained an active interest in education and the advancement of women. She had taught Mary, who laughingly said how she had considered her ancient then.

Thea couldn't remember ever seeing anyone quite so old. Her bed was in a downstairs room with French windows that overlooked the garden and the hills. Her bed was so positioned that she could look up and see everything that she desired. She was dressed in a white cotton nightdress with lace round the neck and cuffs. Her sheets and pillow cases were pristine white and smooth, as was her counterpane. She sat amongst all the whiteness like a piece of frail porcelain, but her eyes had the brightness of a bird and through them her soul shone out.

"Come, my dearest child," she said, beckoning towards Thea. "Come and sit on my bed and tell me all about yourself."

Joy would sit in her pram by the French windows, Mary would relax in the comfy armchair, and Thea would sit on the white counterpane as commanded.

Mrs Douglas's eyes were a smoky grey with white rings round the coloured part and they spoke directly to whoever she was focusing her attention on. "Tell me, dear child," she would say, holding out her fragile hand for the child to grasp, "what are you learning at school? I hope you are learning sensible things that will fit you to be a woman in this world."

"I'm learning all sorts of things," Thea would reply.

"It doesn't matter whether you are good at arithmetic," said the old lady with emphasis in her voice, "are they teaching you an appreciation of history, literature and poetry?"

"I know lots of poetry," said Thea, hoping to please Mrs Douglas. "I know lots of poetry by heart."

"Good," said the old lady, patting Thea's hand. "Tell me, have you read Gray's Elegy?"

"Yes," replied Thea, pleased that a poem that she had studied at school should be mentioned.

Aunty Mary perked up and said, "I remember learning Gray's Elegy."

"Ah yes," said Mrs Douglas, "but do you understand it? What does 'full many a flower is born to blush unseen, and waste its sweetness on the desert air' mean?"

"Well," said Thea with reservation, "does it mean that some flowers bloom but no one ever sees them?"

"Indeed it does," said the old lady, "but really the flowers are people. What the poet is saying is that many people of brilliant talent are never able to show their talents because the situation of their lives doesn't allow their beauty and talent to show, so in fact they live wasted lives."

Thea twiddled the fringe of the counterpane and thought of what Mrs Douglas had said, but the old lady continued, "Don't waste your life, Thea!"

Thea looked up into the aged face, into the bright alert eyes, and said, "I'm going to be really clever, Mrs Douglas."

The old lady chuckled and exclaimed, "There's my girl, that's what I like to hear! Do you know, Thea, I chained myself to the railings of Buckingham Palace with Mrs Pankhurst."

Thea sat up with a start, wondering what Mrs Douglas meant, and considered what an odd statement she had made.

"I was a suffragette," continued Mrs Douglas. "I fought for the freedom of women to be thought individuals in their own right."

Afterwards on their way home across the golf course, Thea questioned her aunt as to what Mrs Douglas meant by the suffragettes and chaining herself to the railings at Buckingham Palace.

"Mrs Douglas was a tremendous character in her day," said Aunty Mary. "Many people thought she was quite cranky, but she felt that men and women should have equal standing in society."

"Why did she chain herself to the railings?" enquired Thea, really puzzled as to why anyone should do such a thing. "I can't see what good chaining yourself to the railings would be."

"Neither could I, my darling, but Mrs Douglas and her friends were aiming to attract attention to the cause and it was a way of getting attention," said Mary.

"I like Mrs Douglas," said Thea. "I would like to see her again. She has such beautiful eyes."

"Do you know," said Mary, "her eyes, when she was younger, were the most beautiful blue. As she has got older they have lost their brilliance, but they are still lovely. I think she is a lesson to us all, but you see she is lucky; although her body is weak, her mind is still alert."

Sometimes Thea and her aunt would visit the Hoopers, who lived towards the far end of the hills. It would be quite a struggle to push the pram up the steep slopes, but the view when they got there was well worthwhile.

Mary would telephone Mrs Hooper to say that they were coming, as unexpected visitors were not generally welcomed.

The Hoopers were, in many ways, a strange couple, who lived a rather isolated life in their rambling house which was perched up on the side of the hill, overlooking the Severn Valley. The house had large windows which peered down haughtily on the houses built further down the hill.

Emma was ten years older than Francis, but because she was in poor health the gap seemed even wider. She was a quiet, unassuming woman with soft grey hair worn in a loose bun at the nape of her neck, mild blue eyes and rather heavy hips. She dressed simply, and wore unfashionable shoes. Francis, on the other hand, was handsome, smartly dressed, neurotic and temperamental. He drove a black Wolseley car and considered himself a cut above ordinary people.

The Hoopers would always make Mary, Thea and the infant most welcome, and give them tea on the terrace if the weather permitted. Otherwise it would be served in the drawing room which had unrivalled views of the valley and the Cotswolds beyond. The cakes were always lovely, but Thea thought that in some way they were a sad couple, living in their eyrie in the hills.

When the weather was sunny, Thea would love to escape from the house and play out of doors with her friends and the other boys and girls from the village. They would play rounders, cricket and tracking, and some days they would spend hours constructing dens in the bracken with the help of dead wood thrown down from the trees in the high winds. Thea particularly liked Lennie, for he was good humoured and reckless, and always presented a challenge. A girl called Molly joined them in the holidays. She was a Londoner who was staying with her grandmother and Thea was given the responsibility of playing with her and introducing her to the village children. She was a nervous girl who had been conditioned to stay in her own garden, for the environment outside was considered dangerous.

The children had a secret hide-out, situated a good distance from the village across several fields. There was a pond fringed by large trees, some of the branches leaning out over the water and others out over the fields. It was here that the children met, exchanged secrets and generally showed off their daring ability at tree climbing and branch swinging.

Thea took Molly there, with a group of children from the village, the aim being to show off and to encourage Molly to be less of a sissy. With catlike agility Thea swung herself up on one of the tall elm trees that had a branch going out at right angles about thirty feet from the earth, and running along the branch she stood fearlessly looking down at the quivering Molly. "Come up," she called. "If I can get up, so can you."

"She's scared," laughed one of the boys. "She's a real sissy, can't even climb a tree."

Molly kept her head bent down, while Thea continued to encourage her to climb the tree and join her on the branch. After a little while Molly stood up and unable to stand the ridicule and scorn any longer began nervously to climb the trunk of the tree.

Iris, thrown into panic by the action and sensing danger, shrieked, "Don't do it Molly. Don't let them talk you into it."

Thea, cajoling softly, said, "There you are, Molly, of course you can do it. Jolly good, Molly, come on, come on."

Molly heaved herself up and clung to the protruding branch, at the end of which sat the smiling Thea. Holding out her arms to Molly, she said, "Come on, run along the branch and join me." There was a distance of about six feet that had to be walked along without anything to hold on to and, mustering all her courage, Molly managed this, as Thea's outstretched arms covered half the distance.

Like an aspen quivering in the wind, Molly clung to Thea at the dangerously elevated position above the laughing faces of the other children. Her face was pale, her hands clammy with nervous perspiration, but she managed a weak smile, feeling for the first time that she was a member of the gang.

The trouble came when the return journey was contemplated, for the bare piece of branch seemed to her as long as the Forth Bridge and she had no idea how she was going to cross it. Thea wriggled herself past, shaking the branch horribly in an attempt to get in front and so provide some sort of anchorage for Molly. Molly, her frail nerves completely shattered, began to howl, loud terrified howls like a trapped hare.

The children stopped their chattering and gazed up into the tree, one or two proffering advice, but mainly they were riveted into immobility by the seriousness of the situation and the awful noise coming from Molly. Iris began to cry silently, sensing impending doom, while Thea cajoled soothingly, but her voice fell on deaf ears, so complete was Molly's terror.

Suddenly Molly slipped, but the hem of her dress caught on to a peg of wood sticking out from the branch and so she fell through her dress and hung for several suspended seconds by the neck of the garment. A couple of boys rushed to the spot where the body hung above them wriggling in its vest and navy-blue knickers, with arms stretched upwards. There was a loud tearing sound as the buttons in the neck tore away and the hem of the dress ripped from the weight, allowing Molly to fall into the waiting arms of one of the boys.

A sigh of relief went through the group and Molly suddenly silenced by the shock sat dazed on the grass in her underclothes. Iris rushed up to her and with great tenderness gathered the frightened girl in her arms, while the others grouped round telling her how lucky she was that she hadn't been strangled.

Thea climbed along the branch and retrieved the sorry remains of the dress. She knew that the incident was entirely her fault and she dreaded to think what Aunty Mary would say.

The dress was certainly beyond repair, for not only was there a ten inch rent above the hem, but the neck was badly torn. At the sight of the dress Molly began to cry, heart-rending sobs rather than terrified shrieks, while Iris patted her back in a gesture of comfort.

"What shall we tell them?" asked Thea. "Shall we say a bull chased you and caught your dress in its horns?"

Lennie let out a guffaw of laughter at the thought of Molly being chased by a bull, but Molly looked up with disbelief at such a lie and said, "I shall say I climbed a tree, because you made me, and I fell down."

"Molly, you can't say that, they will never let you come out to play again," gasped Thea. "We shall have to tell a fib."

"Well, I shan't," choked Molly through her tears. "I promised Mummy that I would never lie."

"Say you fell down the tree, but don't put all the blame on me," begged Thea.

Clarence, one of the boys in the group, had a sister who worked as a housemaid for Miss Davis and he suggested that they should ask her to mend the dress so that it didn't look so awful. If she could fix the buttons and tack along the tear above the hem, it wouldn't look so outstandingly ragged and then the disaster could be slowly broken to the adults. It was generally thought that if Connie would agree to co-operate a slightly repaired dress might ease the situation.

Connie co-operated and laughingly cobbled up the dress and even washed Molly's tear-stained face, but Thea didn't feel very hopeful as they headed towards home, for she knew she would be on the receiving end of the wrath of her indignant aunt and neighbour. Much to Thea's surprise, Molly said she had climbed a tree and slipped, but she made no mention of Thea goading her.

Thea shot her a look of gratitude and immediately the frightened girl went up in her estimation. "Molly isn't used to climbing trees," she said, "and it's easy to slip if you aren't used to it."

Mary gave Thea a piercing look, as if she was well aware of what had really happened, and Thea hoped against hope that no one would notice and comment on the red mark round Molly's neck.

On Friday the first of September the evacuees came pouring into the town. Thea, with a number of school-friends, sat on the wall by the station watching the arrival. Being only ten–year–olds, war meant little to them other than excitement and unexpected drama, as they were not old enough to comprehend the human tragedy of it all.

As the children poured from the train they stood in dazed, obedient lines, labelled like freight being transported to some foreign land. A few talked and laughed noisily and a few sobbed loudly, but the large majority stood silently, accepting whatever it was that fate was about to dish out to them. Organizers ran up and down the lines calling names, while teachers looking hot and flustered tried to group the children. Like drowning people clinging to wreckage, brothers and sisters clung to each other with resolute determination if an attempt was made to separate them.

Fleets of cars, with volunteer drivers, were waiting to take the children to their new homes, and it was when the children were shepherded along, six at a time to the cars, that more tears were shed. Some of the children became very nervous once separated from their friends, imagining in their panic that they would never see them again.

Thea's family had talked a great deal about the possibility of war and Granny in particular was extremely agitated about the whole situation. At school, following the Munich crisis, a service of thanksgiving had been held, so certain was the teacher that war had been averted. However, all hopes and prayers had little effect on Hitler and his Third Reich, as war was now imminent.

Many people had built air raid shelters, cellars had been reinforced, blast walls built and windows criss–crossed with sticky tape in preparation for the awful happening. Granny was certain that Hitler would invade and send them all off to work as slaves in his vineyards, and that everything they ever owned would be destroyed.

A few weeks before, everyone had been fitted for a gas mask and the fearsome, suffocating objects were sitting in their boxes on the cloakroom shelf. Joy had a Mickey Mouse gas mask, but no one had managed to get it anywhere near her face, let alone fixed in position. Aunty Mary hoped that it wouldn't be necessary and anyhow she felt that they would cross that bridge when they got to it.

As soon as the cars began to move, Thea and her friends decided to run to their homes to see what children they had been allotted. The only thing that Mary and Robert had insisted on was that their evacuees should be girls, as the thought of wild, urban boys filled them with dread.

The village was a hive of activity with cars and people everywhere and at every cottage gate someone stood, looking or waiting. As Thea ran along the driveway to the house, her aunt was standing by the gate looking up towards the hills.

"They have arrived," said Thea breathlessly. "We saw them coming off the trains and they are being taken around by car."

"I know," said Mary. It was then that Thea noticed that she was crying. Large tears were rolling down her cheeks but she wasn't bothering to brush them away. It was as though she was crying silently to herself and seemed unaware of the tears.

"What's the matter?" asked Thea. "Why are you crying, Aunty Mary?"

"Poor little things," said Mary, "taken from their homes and pushed into the homes of strangers. How I would hate it if Joy was suddenly taken from me and sent to live with strangers miles away."

She glanced across the lawn to where her daughter was playing, face flushed with the effort of trying to arrange her assortment of dolls into their small pram, and felt doubly grateful that the child was still with her. Thea stood uneasily by her aunt, sensing the tension that had built up within her. The warm late summer sun beat down on them and the afternoon seemed almost explosive with anticipation. Thea realized that possibly life would never be quite the same again and that the quiet order and routine that had ruled their lives would no longer be possible.

Thea touched her aunt's arm and said, "Don't worry, we will take care of them. They will be all right with us, really they will."

Mary smiled weakly, took a handkerchief from her sleeve and wiped her face just as a large black car eased itself slowly along the driveway between the trees.

Quickly pulling herself together, Mary said quickly, "We must look happy. We must make them welcome. You must help me, Thea."

The car stopped and a tall, thin lady carrying a clipboard with papers attached to it got out. Six faces looked out of the back of the car, six grubby, tear-stained faces.

Mary gasped, "I can't take six children," she said. "I shan't be able to cope."

The tall, thin lady laughed. "No, my dear, don't worry, only three of them are for you. Let me see," she looked at her papers, "three girls for you and three for Miss Davis."

"Thank goodness," Mary laughed with relief. "Let me take my little girls then."

Three girls got out of the car, complete with labels and bags, and they stood in a bewildered group by the side of the car. Thea smiled, but they looked back at her vaguely with tired, emotionless faces as though drained of all human responses. Mary chatted to the lady organizer for a moment or two, collecting the details of the girls, and then the car pulled away.

The oldest of the girls was called Jean, a dark-haired, blue-eyed girl of Thea's age. The other two were sisters of seven and eight, thin, mousy-haired girls with large dark eyes. They had been torn from the bosom of their parents with great reluctance, so no amount of persuasion was going to comfort them. They began to weep loudly as they saw the car disappearing and they hardly stopped till their parents collected them a week later.

Aunty Mary decided that Jean should sleep in Thea's room, and she pleaded with her niece for every kindness to be shown, while she struggled to pacify the unhappy sisters. The girls' names were Gwen and Pearl and, although Jean recognized them vaguely as younger members of her school, she didn't know them and so she was no more successful than Mary in trying to get them to settle.

Throughout the night their tormented sobs shook the house, and it was only in the early hours of the morning that peace was restored when the girls snuggled down between Robert and Mary in their double bed and went to sleep. During the day they wouldn't go out of the house, play or eat, but remained in a state of abject grief and despair. When darkness fell the same sobbing began afresh, only ceasing when they were wedged between their unwilling foster parents.

On the third of September the war was declared and Robert's fragile nervous system was almost in shreds, with the lack of sleep, the tension of the crying children and the fear of being blown to pieces any moment causing him to take on again his haunted look of premature old age. A message was got, somehow, to the girls' parents, suggesting that they visit and try if they could to reassure their distraught children.

Exactly a week after the girls had taken up residence in the alien nest, their parents arrived. They were a sad couple, thin, poorly dressed and looking totally out of place in what to them was a strange environment. They had with them a pathetic little boy who was badly spastic, only able to walk with the greatest difficulty and lacking any ability at speech. They had pushed him in a large push chair the two miles from getting off the Birmingham bus, which had exhausted them.

Mary had sufficient reserves of strength to muster a welcome to the bewildered couple, in spite of the fact that she had had very little sleep for the past week. The mother looked so ill with her sallow skin, dark rings under her eyes and straight, greasy hair drawn back from her face and placed into position by numerous grips that Mary felt a tremendous sympathy for her. She made them tea, laying the table with home–made cake, scones and thinly cut bread and butter.

The father, a gaunt, swarthy man, with an almost incomprehensible Black Country accent, sat in an armchair with a daughter on each knee, surveying the scene, while the mother held her handicapped son on her lap, trying hard to control his jerking limbs.

"I've done everything in my power to help them settle," said Mary, "but they haven't eaten anything and they've hardly slept."

"We all sleep together, Missus," replied the mother wearily.

"They ent ust to being on them own."

"I 'aint stopping 'ere," said Pearl firmly, stroking her father's cheek. "I be coming 'ome along of you."

The girls were determined, the parents unable to reason, so in spite of the threat of annihilation by Hitler's bombs the little family went back together to the cosiness of their slum home, somewhere in Birmingham. The girls were actually smiling when they left, in a taxi that Mary had called, as she couldn't stand the thought of them struggling the two miles to catch the bus.

Jean, on the other hand, settled straight away. She was a girl with self-confidence and she seemed to understand the importance and necessity of the evacuation. Her home was in the same poor area of Birmingham, but her parents were sensible and hard-working, so their attitude to life was reflected in their daughter's behaviour.

The day after Gwen and Pearl disappeared with their parents, Jean's family paid a visit. They had not written to say they were coming, and Jean spotted them walking over the common hunting for the house where she had been billeted. She shrieked with delight at the sight of them and Mary told her to go and bring them in, saying good humouredly that she ought to go into the hotel business. Mary made them feel at home, as she did with everyone who entered her house, and she assured them that she was only too delighted for them to visit their daughter whenever they wanted to.

Thea and Jean shared a bedroom and they gained a great deal from each other's company. Jean was much more worldly than Thea, having gained her experience in the urban streets. She had a strongly developed survival instinct, was not easily cowed and didn't frighten easily. Thea on the other hand was inclined to be afraid of people and could never cope with aggression or argument, but she understood her own country environment.

Jean attended the local church school, part-time to begin with, but after a few weeks the situation sorted itself out, as many of the original evacuees had returned to Birmingham, so full-time schooling became possible. Everyone had expected the bombing of the big cities to begin straight away, so when it hadn't happened, some people felt that the war was phoney, and that it was unnecessary to have their families divided, so they gathered their children together and went back to resume living their lives in the crowded streets.

Jean made no mention of ever wanting to return, seeming to prefer the calm of the countryside to the noisy warmth of her family's back-to-back house, although she dearly loved her family, and they in return loved her.

Mary, Robert and Joy formed their own family unit, and in many ways Thea felt apart, so in Jean she sensed a kindred spirit. Robert made no secret of the fact that he would much prefer to live quietly with his wife and daughter and, although never unkind, he was often indifferent. Thea knew that Joy was the most precious thing in the world to Uncle Robert, but his over-protectiveness at times reached irritating levels. Mary, on the other hand, tried desperately to share her affection around, although of course as Joy was so young she received a great deal of her mother's attention.

While Mary and Robert's household was settling down to normality following the upheaval of the first week of war, Granny and Aunty Margaret were having a very stressful time. About ten days after the outbreak of war, Aunty Margaret arrived at her sister's house in a rather anguished state. Flinging herself into an armchair, much to everyone's astonishment she burst into tears.

Unused to seeing her sister ruffled, Mary was quite alarmed by the outburst and enquired tenderly what the bother was.

"It's just too bad," sniffed Margaret. "She thinks just because the war has broken out that she can completely control our lives."

"Who, my darling?" enquired Mary, putting her arms round her sister. "Who wants to control your life?"

Margaret lifted a blotched, distressed face to her sister and said, "That beastly cat, Aunt Julia, and her wishy-washy daughter, Sophie."

"What!" exclaimed Mary. "You mean they are with you and Mother?"

Robert was out, but Thea and Jean sat tensely, caught by the drama of the situation.

Margaret blew her nose fiercely and said hoarsely, "Do you know, on the Sunday that war was declared, Mother and I were preparing dinner and suddenly a car stopped at the gate and as large as life out got Aunt Julia and Sophie and started unloading trunks out of the car. They announced that they had arrived for the duration of the war—which they expected to be over by Christmas—but as they

were family they thought we would rather have them than unknown evacuees billeted on us."

"Didn't they ask?" blurted out the astonished Mary. "You mean
they just expected you to have them?"

Margaret dried her tears and her expression became more angry
than upset. "It wouldn't be so bad," she continued, "if they helped,
but they expect Mother and me to wait on them. Also they demand
separate bedrooms." Margaret got up from the chair and walked
towards the window. "God forgive me," she said with feeling, "but I
really hate the old bitch, walking round with her blessed jewel box."

Thea sat up, for already she was quite excited by the image of
Aunt Julia, and words like cat and bitch being thrown about were so
out of character for her prim aunt that she felt that Aunty Julia must
be beastly indeed. She gave Jean a little dig on the thigh and they
exchanged sly smiles.

"Jewel box!" Mary exclaimed. "You mean she has a box full of
jewels?"

Margaret sniffed with disapproval and threw her head back in
contempt. "I don't know what's in the stupid box," she said, "but she
won't leave it anywhere, not even in the bedroom. Anyone would
think the house was running with thieves."

"They will get fed up," said Mary soothingly. "The war is a
novelty at the moment, but they will soon want to go back to their
own home. Give it another week, dear, and you will see, they will
leave as quickly as they came."

"It's not as if they ever cared much for us," continued Margaret,
"and what's more they are making Mother ill." She threw in the
final statement like a trump card, knowing that Mary would be
stirred by that information if by no other.

"We are not having Mother made ill," Mary said. "Aunt Julia and
Sophie must help. If they are not prepared to help, then they must
go. I will tell Aunt Julia myself."

"I tell you what," said Mary, as another splendid idea flooded into
her head, "you and Mother come and stay here for a few days and
leave them on their own. Don't bother to get any shopping in—let
them cope!"

A smile of satisfaction played around Margaret's lips, as though
her sister's idea was quite acceptable and might possibly do the trick

of upsetting Aunt Julia's equilibrium. Thea, who couldn't contain her curiosity any longer, enquired who Aunt Julia was.

"The old so-and-so is your grandmother's late brother's widow," said Aunty Margaret, "and Sophie is her daughter, but she is the most spineless individual I have ever met and Aunt Julia is the most arrogant."

Aunty Margaret stayed for tea and the conversation continued on endlessly about Aunt Julia and Sophie and their odd ways. In the end their peculiarities became amusing and everyone began to laugh. The jewel box became an object of hilarity and Aunt Julia's lorgnette so funny that tears were running down everyone's cheeks. Poor Sophie's simpering mannerisms were mimicked by Aunty Margaret and by the end of the meal she felt a whole lot better.

In spite of the inspired ideas meant to uproot Aunt Julia and the snide remarks intended to cut her to the quick, a month after the outbreak of war she and her daughter were still firmly entrenched with Granny and Aunt Margaret even though the latter's nerves and frayed tempers were getting the better of them. Robert, in the end, came to the rescue. A friend of his was willing to let part of his house, as his wife had recently died. Aunt Julia was persuaded that a self-contained flat would suit her much better and that she was free to visit her sister-in-law and niece whenever she chose to.

With a good deal of grumbling and remarks such as "Not even your family can help you in a crisis," Aunt Julia and Sophie piled all their belongings into a taxi and moved into the self-contained furnished flat. They were hurt, and they made no attempt to hide their bruised feelings. Aunt Julia's final remark was, "I am glad your brother is not alive to see this day." As the car disappeared down the road, Granny was heard to mutter, "I should think it was you who sent him to his early grave."

On a golden October afternoon about six weeks after war had been declared, Thea with Jean, Mavis and Iris were sitting in a patch of bronzed bracken against a wood of larch trees on the side of the hills. It was one of the rare, jewelled days of autumn when summer seemed to have returned for a visit, but the air had an autumnal sweetness about it with the sky washed clear by the previous night's rain.

"It's so beautiful," remarked Thea, "but it may not last . . ."

"Why?" Iris sat up, her hazel eyes wide with apprehension.

"Because Hitler might have killed us all," said Thea. "He could shoot and bomb us all and that would be the end of us."

"Don't be daft," said Jean. "He won't bother to kill us!" She was chewing a piece of grass as she lay on her back looking up at the cloudless sky.

Mavis, serious and philosophical as ever, said with the calm assurance of someone who had read and thought a great deal about the matter, "It is possible that we shall be invaded by Germany, but I don't think we shall all be killed, because I can't think what Hitler would gain from that."

"God wouldn't let us be killed," exclaimed Iris. "I know He loves us too much."

Thea turned and looked at her friend with surprise. Gentle, naïve Iris who only ever thought of the nice things in life and refused to consider anything horrid or evil. "You are stupid sometimes, Iris," Thea said. "What do you mean, God won't let it happen?"

"Well, He won't," replied Iris defensively.

"And what do you think God is?" asked Thea of her friend. "Do you think He is some sort of man playing a game with us all and who says, 'I'll let the English win because I like them best?' Really Iris, what do you understand by God?"

Iris dug her finger into the peaty soil underneath a root of bracken and, without looking at Thea, said, "Well, He is God. The God who is in the Bible."

"Everyone has different ideas of God," said Mavis. "There is no right or wrong idea, just different ideas."

Jean brought a breath of earthiness into the conversation by saying, "I think you lot talk a load of tripe."

"You can't be bothered to think," retorted Thea. "It's easy to say things are tripe when you don't stop to consider them."

"Anyhow," said Mavis, looking thoughtfully into the valley with a distant wondering expression in her eyes, "God is love. The Devil is evil. Man is evil when he makes war. That's all I know."

The girls were silent, each wrapped in their own thoughts. A honeyed breeze rustled the bracken and sighed through the branches of the larch trees. The valley, green and gold, stretching before them made war and destruction seem a long way away.

Chapter Nine

I N the golden heat of high summer Thea was eleven years old and the war was no longer phoney, but a gripping, terrifying reality. With the fall of France an invasion by Germany became a horrible possibility. The future was uncertain and a heavy cloud hung over everyday living. In September the Battle of Britain raged and fearful accounts of the losses were on the front pages of every newspaper. Mr Churchill's voice boomed out encouragement from the wireless, but many people were beginning to lose heart.

In mid September Mabel arrived at Mary's house unexpectedly. She was pale and tearful and shut herself in the bedroom.

"Leave her," commanded Mary. "She must get over her grief. She has lost friends that mean a lot to her. She needs a few weeks complete rest here with us."

Thea accepted Mary's advice and within a few days Mabel was mixing with the family again. Thea rarely had conversations with her, but on the odd occasions she did call her Mum, to please her aunt.

One day, shortly after Mabel had arrived for her rest with her sister, Thea went shopping with her and they met an elderly teacher who had taught her and her sisters.

The elderly teacher greeted Mabel warmly and said, "How lovely to see you Mabel, and to meet your daughter."

"She isn't my daughter," replied Mabel quickly, as if anxious to dispel any such notions. "She is an evacuee living with my sister."

"Silly me," exclaimed the teacher. "I thought I could see a family likeness. It is amazing how one can be tricked into seeing likenesses."

Thea gasped, for she couldn't believe that Mabel had denied her so utterly, and a hot sick feeling surged through her body.

Mabel took a sixpence from her handbag, pressed it into Thea's hand saying, "Go and get yourself an ice cream, while I have a little chat with Miss Smith."

Thea crossed the road to walk towards the shop, but ice cream didn't interest her. She felt like a dog that had just been thrown out of the house by its owner. As she sat down dejectedly on the wide window-sill of the shop, she could see Mabel talking to Miss Smith, but that made her feel even more miserable and resentful.

"One day," she muttered to herself, "I'm going to be important. Mabel will then be proud of me and be pleased to introduce me as her daughter."

Sitting alone in the sunshine, Thea tried to think how she could achieve fame. She decided that she would work hard at school, and become so clever, cleverer than anyone else in the family, then she would become famous. She pictured herself in a lovely house with a handsome husband entertaining her admiring family. She had decided that perhaps she would get married after all, after she had achieved her aim of becoming a doctor.

It was a purely feminine group that set out for the hills for a picnic. There was Aunty Mary with Joy, Aunty Margaret with Molly, Mabel, Jean, Iris, Mavis and Thea. Granny had decided that she was too old for picnics at the end of September.

They caught the bus and went to the terminus towards the southern end of the hills, and then made their way up the steep winding path, clutching baskets, rugs and all the endless paraphernalia of a picnic. They walked for a while along the paths, but the sun was warm, and their burdens heavy, they found a suitable spot where the grass was soft with shade thrown from a large sycamore tree, and settled down.

"That's the Hoopers' house," said Thea, recognising a large house below them on the side of the hill. "We haven't visited them for quite a while."

"Mrs Hooper is dead," said Mary sadly. "Last January it was. She was fixing a black-out curtain on the landing window, and she fell off the ladder and down the stairs."

"How dreadful," exclaimed Margaret. "Did she break her neck?"

"I'm not sure," replied Mary. "I think she might have had a stroke which caused the fall, but I don't know, and I haven't visited Francis."

"Poor thing," said Thea shivering slightly. She looked down at the house and thought of dowdy Emma in her huge house with its voluptuous garden, but it was difficult to comprehend that she was dead.

The picnic things were spread out on the grass while Iris flicked the late wasps with a magazine. The sandwiches and cakes were placed on the rug. There was home-made ginger beer, tea and milk kept hot or cold, whichever was required, in thermos flasks. Aunty Mary had made a fruit cake which was sitting resplendent in a large tin. Just as everyone was tucking into the food, a heavy black cloud appeared in the valley.

"Heavens, we are going to have a storm," said Aunty Margaret in a doom-laden voice. "Just when we've got everything settled."

"It will pass," spluttered Mabel, her mouth full of food.

"Look, you can see it is going to follow the line of the river."

She had no sooner spoken than a streak of forked lightning flashed down the sky, followed by a loud crack of thunder. The sun was still shining where they were sitting, but a dark curtain of rain hung from the heavy cloud as it moved steadily across the valley.

"I think we shall have to be prepared to move," said Mary, "otherwise we shall get soaked if this breaks on us."

Another flash of lightning settled the question. The picnic things were hastily repacked.

"I want my cake," shrieked Joy. "Where are we going to go?"

"I tell you what," said Mary, "Let's ask Francis Hooper if we can shelter there until the storm passes. I don't think he would mind."

Everybody was given something to carry, and they made their way quickly down the steeper path which led directly to the house. The valley continued to shake and resound with the large clashes of thunder, and the angry blue-white streaks tore at the sky. The sun suddenly vanished from view, and the first large spots fell as they reached the driveway.

"You stay here," commanded Mary urgently, "while I go and ring the bell and see if he minds."

"Thank goodness Mary knows someone," said Mabel, glancing up at the sky. "Who is he anyhow?"

Mary with Joy in hand ran up the driveway, climbed the steps and anxiously rang the bell. The group at the bottom of the drive-way waited apprehensively, as the spots of rain were increasing, and they feared that Francis might not be in.

The door opened and Mary could be seen talking. Then she turned towards them, beckoning for them to go into the house. With noisy excitement the girls rushed up the driveway, followed by Mabel and Margaret, just as the heavens opened and rain in torrents fell from the sky. They bunched into the hall nearly knocking the astonished Francis over in their anxiety to get out of the rain.

"I didn't realize there were so many of you," exclaimed Francis, leaning against the banisters. "You had better come into the kitchen and spread your things on the table."

It was only when they were in the kitchen and their arms free of objects that anyone really noticed Francis. In spite of the warmness of the day, he was dressed in a clerical grey suit complete with white shirt and black tie. His face was like parchment and he looked terribly ill and thin.

Mary almost gasped in surprise and said, "You don't look well, Francis."

"I'm not well," he replied. "Since Emma passed on I have been terribly ill. I can't be bothered to cook, so I hardly eat anything. I have lost three stone." He gave the information in an almost elated voice, courting sympathy.

The girls sat down around the kitchen table with the remains of the picnic piled in front of them. Mabel looked out of the window at the fury of the thunderstorm, while Margaret leaned against the kitchen dresser, looking, like her sister, at the shadow of the man that had been Francis Hooper.

"You still run your business?" enquired Mary.

Francis shook his head. "No," he replied. "I have given everything up. My heart is too weak to carry on. Everything is a real mess and this place is going to pot. I can't get a proper gardener, only a handyman, and this garden is too much for me."

"Come and share tea with us," said Margaret, trying to force gaiety into her voice, for the man was beginning to depress her.

The food was spread on the big kitchen table and the semblance of the picnic began to reappear. Mary asked Francis for a large plate so that the cake could be freed from its tin and take pride of place in the centre of the table. There were plenty of sandwiches, scones and cakes. Francis put on the kettle saying that he would make a pot of tea, as thermos flask tea never tasted quite right. He recounted the unhappy events which had led to Emma's death, and the adults were duly stunned by the awfulness of the happening.

The girls chatted together, ate sandwiches, giggled and drank ginger beer before going out into the garden, for the storm had disappeared as quickly as it had arrived. They left the grown-ups sitting round the table wrapped in morbid conversation.

"They love death," said Thea contemptuously. "Illness and death really get them going. Come on, let's explore his garden."

Holding Joy's hand, the girls pushed their way through the shrubbery, across mossy lawns flanked by rather weedy flower beds, through the cherry orchard to the summer house, which was situated at the highest point of the garden looking down the valley like a superior old lady. By the summer house a spring spurted from the rock face and ran into an ornamental pool which overflowed in a series of steps and miniature waterfalls into another larger pool containing goldfish of the most enormous size.

The girls sat in the summer house and giggled at each other with pleasure, for they felt as if they had found a secret garden. Rain dripped from the trees. The grass sparkled like a thousand diamonds. The valley was clear and washed, making everything smell fresh and lovely.

"Does he sit up here on his own?" enquired Mavis. "It's like something out of a fairy story, a sort of enchanted garden."

Thea shrugged her shoulders. "I don't know," she said. "Aunty Mary and I used to come and have tea with them sometimes. Shall I go and get some ginger beer and bring it up here?"

"That's a good idea," said Jean. "See if you can bring some cake if there's any left."

After a little while Thea left them and made her way back towards the house. The garden felt remote and secretive, with a kind of haunting sadness because there was no one but the ill, lonely man to walk among the lovely shrubs and trees. Birds sang un-molested and butterflies flitted undisturbed amongst the flowers, and from the stone walls which had been built to terrace some of the garden valerian in large rose-red bunches hung against the pink-grey rocks.

She entered the house from the door which led from the terrace straight into the kitchen and she saw her two aunts standing by the sink washing up the cups and saucers.

"Is there any ginger beer left?" she asked. "We are sitting in the summer house and the others thought it would be nice to have a drink."

"Possibly. Shake the thermos flask and see," said Mary, looking momentarily at her niece and then resuming her wiping up.

Thea walked across the kitchen floor, noticing with a start that her mother and Mr Hooper were still sitting at the table, but Mr Hooper's arm was spread right round her mother's chair and his face was pressed very close to her hair. As Thea picked up the flasks, she noticed that her mother was smiling and she had an excited, girlish expression in her eyes. They were wrapped up in each other and seemed hardly aware of Thea standing by the table.

Thea picked up the flasks and cups and started to go towards the terrace door. "We are in the summer house," she called. No one answered her, for her aunts were deep in conversation and her mother was otherwise engaged. Almost running in her eagerness to join her friends, she sped through the garden, arriving panting at the summer house.

"She is flirting with him," she burst out.

Jean had been telling the others a funny story and they were shrieking with laughter as Thea arrived. They stopped suddenly at Thea's statement, and Iris said, "Who is flirting with who?"

"My mother is flirting with Mr Hooper," stated Thea violently. "An hour ago she didn't know him, and now she is flirting with him."

"Oh go on, let her have her fun," laughed Jean. "Don't be an old spoil sport."

Thea ignored Jean's remark, and putting the flasks down on the summer house floor said, "My mother makes me cross."

"I thought he was dying," said Mavis. "A bit of a quick recovery if he is able to flirt."

Thea made a gesture with her hands indicating perplexity and walked over to where her young cousin was leaning over the pool playing with the goldfish. The fish were swimming in the shade of the water lily leaves and then into the sunlight where their gold bodies sparkled in the silver of the water. Molly joined them, lying on the grass, her hands in the coolness of the water.

Molly, although highly strung, was perceptive of other people's feelings. "The thunderstorm has spoilt the picnic for you, hasn't it?"

She glanced at Thea nervously, feeling that the day had been ruined for her.

"You can't choose weather," retorted Thea. "I would have liked it not to have rained, but there it is."

"Didn't you want to come here?"

"No, I would like to have stayed on the hill." Thea smiled at Molly, for she knew that Molly was kind and understanding, even though she was a bit soppy.

On the way home on the bus and walking across the common, the conversation was varied, but little mention was made of Mr Hooper. They all decided another picnic would be a good idea, but they didn't think it likely as it was so late in the year.

It was early in October when Mary gave Thea the startling news. "Your mother is going to marry Mr Hooper," she said.

Thea was packing her school books into a satchel, and for a few seconds was stunned by what her aunt had said. She looked across the breakfast room to where Mary was stacking up the cereal bowls so calmly, as though what she had just said was an everyday statement.

"My mother, to marry Mr Hooper?" Thea stuttered. "But she doesn't know him. She has only met him once." As she spoke she felt her legs going weak. She felt that she would become involved in this unlikely liaison.

"She has seen quite a lot of him," said Mary. "Anyhow, they have decided to marry."

"Why?" Thea asked in an astounded voice.

"I suppose they get on well," replied Mary. "Your mother must get out of the bombing, her nerves are in shreds. Another thing, he is so lonely, so sick, he must have someone to care for him."

None of the reasons given by her aunt seemed a satisfactory explanation as to why anyone should marry. Mr Hooper of all people, Thea felt, was a strange choice. "She will give up her flat in Birmingham, I suppose?" Thea asked.

Mary nodded her head. "We will talk about it this evening," she said. "You will be late if you don't get your things together and start on your way."

Thea ran along the driveway hardly comprehending what her aunt had said. She longed to tell Iris and see what she thought about it. All her mother's friends had been so witty and smart that she found it difficult to understand why she had chosen Mr Hooper for a husband. Strange, ill, melancholy Mr Hooper, who lived in the lovely house on the hill, alone among his trees with only his fan-tail pigeons for company.

She had been late for school before Aunty Mary had given her the news and now she was even later than ever, running with legs that refused to gather any speed.

On arrival at school everyone was going into the assembly hall. Throwing her books down in the class room, Thea grabbed a piece of paper and on it she wrote, "My mother is going to marry Mr Hooper." She knew she wouldn't be seated near to Iris, but at least she could pass the message to her.

"You've missed the register," said the teacher.

Thea mumbled her apology and followed the other girls into the hall. She spotted Iris three rows in front of her, so she tapped the arm of the girl in the next row and whispered, "Pass to Iris." In spite of the Head's stern stare from the platform, the sacred music coming from the piano, the general air of discipline, all she wanted was Iris to acknowledge the message.

They were half way through the hymn before the paper reached Iris. She read it, turned, pulled a face denoting surprise at Thea, folded the paper, put it into her gymslip pocket and proceeded to sing the rest of the hymn. It was not until the mid-morning break that Thea could receive Iris's opinion and then they had to wait until they were away from the other girls in a quiet place.

"Do you really think they have fallen in love?" gasped Iris. "He is years older than your mother."

"Aunty Mary said something about her wanting to get away from the bombing," replied Thea, "and him wanting someone to look after him."

Iris was serious, her large hazel eyes round with dismay. "You'll have to live with them," she announced. "They are bound to want you to live with them."

The possibility of leaving Aunty Mary hadn't entered Thea's head, so Iris's words made her heart thump with apprehension. "I shan't go," she said firmly. "It's her funeral if she marries him, but I'm not going."

Iris twanged the wire netting surrounding the playground with her fingers. "Once he has married your mother," she stated seriously, "I think he is in charge."

The bell interrupted their conversation so they were forced back into the class room, but Thea found it difficult to concentrate on the algebra lesson. The teacher's voice chirped on merrily, but all she could think of was the big gloomy house on the side of the hill, the pale sick man and the weird, enchanted garden. The thought of him suddenly being in charge of her was unbelievable; she felt sure that Iris must be wrong, for how could someone that she hardly knew be in charge of her?

When Thea arrived home from school, Aunty Mary informed her that her mother and Mr Hooper were to marry the following week. It was to be a quiet affair, in a registry office, no fuss at all. A van was collecting the things from the flat in Birmingham. The question of Thea's future had not been discussed, but she supposed it would be in due time.

Thea went to her bedroom, threw her school books on the floor and lay on her bed. Jean wasn't back from school so the room was her own for a while. She hated the thought of people discussing her future, for it made her feel like an object that had to be considered. Other people lived in settled ordinary families, their future certain. Not for the first time she wished she was grown up and able to decide her own future. This endless embarrassment because she was alive was mortifying. From her bedroom window the comforting line of the hills was visible and she watched a cloud drifting like a silver edged island across the crest of the hill. She decided that the following day after school she would visit her grandmother and discuss the situation with her. If anyone would understand it would be Gran, as she was always full of gentle unemotional advice.

The next morning before Thea set out for school, she checked with her aunt that it would be convenient to visit Granny, but she knew that no objection would be made as Mary was always pleased if her mother had company, for she knew that she got lonely. Mary visited her as often as she could, but it was really too far to walk and the bus journey was not straightforward, as the bus had to be changed and long waits were often involved in the change-over.

When Thea got to her grandmother's house in the late afternoon, she found her on her own as Aunty Margaret was still at work. She was sitting in her armchair by the fire, dressed in a grey silk dress with a soft white shawl round her shoulders. She looked up at Thea with definite pleasure as she entered the room.

"My dear child," she said, "how lovely to see you. Come along and sit by the fire. It feels chilly today. Is it still raining?"

Thea shook her head, and bent down and kissed her grandmother. Her face felt soft and smelt of lavender.

"She is going to marry Mr Hooper, Gran," Thea said, bending down by the fender and picking up the poker to rake the fire. She glanced at her grandmother to see what reaction her statement made, but the old lady didn't say anything but just made a fatalistic gesture with her hands.

"Are you pleased, Gran?" Thea kept her eyes fixed on her grandmother's face. The bluey-grey, deep set eyes seemed filled with sadness.

"I don't know, child," came the reply. "I don't know." She touched her hair vaguely with her hand, pushing the fine white strands back from her face. Her hair was as fine as silk and had an almost gossamer quality to it.

Thea put her hand on her grandmother's knee and said, "Have you met him?"

The old lady patted Thea's hand in a reassuring manner and then held out her hand lightly. Thea noticed how fragile her grandmother's hands were; the skin as delicate as tissue paper with the pale blueness of the veins showing through.

"I have met him, child," she said gently. "Mabel took me to meet him. We had tea together."

"And?" Thea looked questioningly into the wise face.

"He seemed very pleasant," came the reply, "but whether he is right for your mother I can't tell. I never did understand Mabel; she was always so difficult to understand." The old lady sighed as though suddenly the world was too much for her and people's behaviour beyond her understanding.

For a few moments the room was silent, the only sound coming from the melancholy ticking of the grandfather clock. Thea still held on to her grandmother's hand and she stroked the pale skin gently. "Will it make any difference to me, Gran?" she asked.

"I should think you'll stay with Aunty Mary," replied Granny. "Your mother's allowance will stop, of course."

"Allowance! What allowance?"

"Your mother had an allowance from your father."

"Why?" the question was direct and penetrating.

"Because he couldn't marry your mother he gave her an allowance."

Thea, suddenly thrown by talk of her father, said, "Why couldn't he marry her?"

"He was married with children, hadn't you been told?"

"I don't know anything about him," Thea said quietly.

"Well," continued Granny, "now he has been killed the allowance has stopped, so your mother needs support."

"Killed!" the strange word stabbed into Thea's heart. She never imagined that she had a father, she thought she had been born without one, for there had never been a mention of him before.

Granny looked up with her pale, sad eyes. "I didn't know him child, it's just that I know he has been shot down in his Spitfire over Kent and that he didn't survive."

Thea sat back on her heels in amazement. The notion of a father in a Spitfire was hard to assimilate. She tried hard but no image would come to mind.

"It will stop your mother longing," continued Granny. "She pinned so many hopes on him. She always thought that he would divorce his wife and marry her." Granny leant forward towards Thea. "I never thought he would divorce his wife; it would bring too much disgrace on to his family. I always thought it was a pipe dream on Mabel's part."

Thea just stared at her grandmother for she really had little comprehension of what she was talking about. Never before had her father been mentioned, so there wasn't even a shadow or a dream figure to cling to.

"It's best," said the old lady, pursing her lips in a gesture of finality. "It's best that she marries and forgets her past."

She caught Thea's eye in her gaze. "I know child that you are part of her past, and that every time she looks at you she will be reminded, but it's best that she has a fresh start."

A dreadful feeling of guilt whelmed up in the pit of Thea's stomach, for she knew she was responsible for this awful thing that had embarrassed her family. A lump rose in her throat. "Am I bad, Gran," she choked. "Should I never have been born?"

Granny sighed, as if the world had thrown its burden on her tired, old shoulders. "You're not bad my dear, it's not your fault; it's your mother's fault."

She longed to ask if it was her father's fault too, but she didn't for Granny had said he was dead. The teacher at school had talked about the Battle of Britain and the wonderful airmen who were keeping Britain safe from the Germans. In a way, the strange unknown man in his Spitfire—a hero—was her father. She wouldn't be able to tell anyone about him, and she had no idea what he looked like, or in fact his name, but somewhere deeply inside her was a little warm feeling of pride.

"What was his name, Gran?"

Granny shook her head. "I've no idea child, you'll have to ask your mother."

"I couldn't do that Gran, I wouldn't know what to say."

Granny smiled. "Well then don't bother. Does it really matter what his name was?"

Thea felt a great surge of love, mixed with pity for her grand-mother, who looked so frail and vulnerable that Thea felt that she ought to be cared for and protected rather than worried by other people's problems.

Standing on a table by the window was a large cut glass vase containing amber and gold chrysanthemums. The light catching the prisms sent a shower of rainbow diamonds across the polished surface of the table. Thea stroked the moist velvet petals, moving her fingers from the tight centres outwards over the curved surface of the flowers. She put her face into the blooms but there was no real scent, just a strange, musty earthiness, and she wondered how such a lovely flower could be scentless.

Granny opened her eyes, turning her head towards Thea and the flowers. "He brings them in from the garden," she said, "but I don't really like them."

"Why, Gran?" The child looked puzzled.

"They smell of death," said the old lady sadly. "They smell of autumn, decay and death. I would rather have the summer flowers." She sat up in her chair and, smiling at Thea, said, "All autumn flowers aren't sad. I like the dahlias and the Michaelmas daisies, but chrysanthemums I don't like, I suppose because they remind me of funerals. But he will bring them in."

"He is so old," said Thea, thinking of the grey-faced old man who tidied up Granny's garden.

"Old and obstinate." Granny gave a little laugh. "He grows what he wants, you know, not what I want. He will never be told. He says, 'Yes ma'am', but he does exactly as he pleases."

A voice called cheerily from the kitchen and Granny got up, straightened her shawl, patted her hair, and said, "Well, here is your Aunty Margaret home for tea. Thank goodness for the evening and your aunt's company."

It was several weeks after the marriage that Thea was invited to visit her mother and Mr Hooper.

"They want you to go for the weekend," said Aunty Mary. "That will be nice for you, for you can get to know them. They might of course bring up the question of you living with them, so you must be prepared."

Thea was horrified. "I'm not going to live with them. I couldn't live there, with them!"

Mary shrugged her shoulders. "The question will arise," she said. "Francis says he won't keep you while you are living with me. I don't mind; I don't want payment for you. I would much rather you stayed with me." She smiled at her niece reassuringly. "I am just warning you, dear. Uncle Robert says that you ought to go, but I think you should stay here."

Aunty Mary's words made Thea feel depressed and down-hearted, so it was a rather reluctant girl that got off the bus and made her way up the steep path and along the hillside road to the house. She couldn't help but think of the occasions when she had visited the Hoopers with her aunt and how little they had meant to her then. Now, suddenly, Mr Hooper was her stepfather and her mother was living at the house.

As Thea walked up the driveway, she noticed that Mabel was standing by the drawing room window and, when she saw Thea, she waved excitedly. By the time she had reached the top of the steps the front door was open and Mabel was calling to her in an exclamation of welcome. "My darling, how are you?"

Thea, unused to such endearments from her mother, was quite taken aback by the greeting. Mr Hooper was standing in the shadow further along the hall, and as Thea stepped through the door he came forward with his arms stretched out in welcome.

"Thea, my dear," he said. "I am glad you have come."

Thea smiled and put her hand out towards his. She noticed how different he looked, so much fatter, healthier and younger looking. He was dressed in green tweed with a lighter green check shirt.

Mabel grabbed his arm as they stood together beaming at Thea. "Well, our little girl has come to visit us," she said. "Isn't that delightful?"

Thea was ushered into the drawing room, feeling strangely elated by the affectionate greeting, but at the same time oddly alarmed by it. She noticed straight away that the room looked different, for the room that had previously been cluttered with Victoriana was transformed into a light, enchanting room.

Mr Hooper, noticing the surprise in Thea's face, said, "It's your mother that's done it. Quite a genius she is at rearranging things." He put his arms round his wife's shoulders and gave her a hug, and she gazed up at him affectionately.

"Sit down, my dear," he said to Thea, patting an armchair by the fire, "and we will have tea."

Mabel pulled in the tea trolley from the kitchen and Thea recognized it from the Birmingham flat. Some of the paintings she also knew and a number of the silver framed photographs, which had been rehoused on the marble mantelpiece.

Thea smoothed the pleats of her gymslip and placed the napkin on her knee. She had come straight from school, as the bus to the southern end of the hills ran very close to her school. She had hoped to change into a dress for tea, but tea had obviously been prepared and they were waiting for her to arrive before they began.

"Now, little Thea," said Mr Hooper kindly, "you must call me Papa. I can't have you calling me Mr Hooper."

Thea had got her mouth full of bread and butter, so she couldn't reply, but a feeling of embarrassment and horror went through her. She smiled at Mr Hooper as though in acknowledgement, but the thought of calling him Papa was quite inconceivable. She had only recently got over the obstacle of calling Mabel, Mum, and that had been fraught with problems.

"We want you to be our little girl," said Mabel cheerily. "We have a nice home here, and there is no reason at all why you shouldn't live here with us."

Thea took another large bite of bread and butter to avoid having to answer, and she smiled at them over the crust to avoid her confusion.

"It's early days yet," said Mr Hooper, "but we want you to think about it and get used to the idea."

The conversation was changed and they asked her about school, her friends, her hobbies, in fact everything they thought would interest her. After tea she was shown her bedroom, which had a window looking out on to the side of the hill. Mr Hooper had placed quite a number of books on the chest of drawers, which he felt might interest her, and on a table by the side of the bed was a wireless.

"I thought you would like that," he said, beaming with pleasure. "You can lie in bed and listen to music or stories."

Thea didn't know what to say, for she had never dreamt of having a wireless all to herself. Uncle Robert had a wireless but it was only ever put on for the news. Occasionally Aunty Mary had switched it on and listened to some music, but it was always turned off when Uncle Robert came home.

"There are ear phones too," said Mr Hooper, "so you can listen in bed without disturbing anyone else."

Thea was enthralled, and she couldn't think of any of her friends who had a wireless of their own. She couldn't wait to tell them on Monday. After she had bathed she lay in bed with the wireless on and the ear phones in position listening to music and songs. She switched off when she heard Mabel and Francis going to bed, feeling that it must be very late. Their room was across a small landing from where she was sleeping and she could hear them chatting as they bathed and prepared for bed.

After a little while the house was plunged into a silence that Thea had never experienced before. The blackness, the strangeness of everything seemed to press down on her. She couldn't sleep, even though she felt very tired, but instead she tossed and turned miserably, wishing she could hear Jean breathing heavily in her heavy adenoidal sleep or Uncle Robert giving his thin cough.

The bedroom had two doors, one going on to the landing from which her room led and the other leading on to a passage that ran from one of the bathrooms. As she lay there, she was sure she heard footsteps in the passageway outside her door. They were soft footsteps going along from her room in the direction of the bathroom. Paralysed with terror she clutched the pillow, but she didn't dare call out. Instead she waited for the footsteps to return, but they didn't return, only the terrible suffocating silence and blackness.

Just before dawn she dropped off to sleep and, when Francis appeared in his dressing gown at her bedroom door, she woke with a start for she was in a very heavy sleep. "Come into our room and have your tea," he said.

Thea rubbed her eyes and stumbled into their bedroom, feeling that she must do as Francis asked. Their room was spacious with three large windows each looking out on to a different vista. Mabel was sitting up in bed wearing a pretty lavender silk nightdress, propped up by a number of pillows.

She pulled the sheet back invitingly. "Come on, snuggle down with us," she said. "Have you slept well? You still look sleepy."

Thea climbed into bed by the side of Mabel wishing that she could have stayed in her own bed for several more hours, now that it was daylight. "Who used to sleep in my room?" she asked.

Francis, handing her a cup of tea, looked surprised at her question. "Why do you ask?" he said.

"Just wondered," said Thea, considering whether she ought to mention the footsteps.

"Old Ma used to sleep there," Francis replied. "Old Ma, Emma's mother. That was her room until she died. As a matter of fact she died in that room. Lovely old lady."

Thea shivered as she sipped her tea. A great feeling of foreboding overcame her. The thought of someone dying where she had slept filled her with fear.

"Can I sleep in another room?" Thea asked, trying to contain the fear that was building up in her throat. "Can I sleep in a room that looks down the valley?"

Mabel laughed and said, "That's a lovely room that you have. I chose it especially for you. Because someone has died in a room makes no difference, you silly Billy."

"I heard footsteps in the night," said Thea quietly, continuing to sip her tea. "They were in the passage."

Francis was sitting on the side of the bed pouring himself out another cup of tea. He looked at Thea kindly and said, "It was the wind whistling under the floorboards. It can happen in a house like this because it is so high up the hill. Every little sound is magnified, my dear, but you mustn't interpret sounds made by the wind into footsteps as that is silly."

The sun was pouring through the windows and glowing on the amber coloured trees, so indeed to think of darkness and footsteps was silly, for such ghosts of the night seemed ridiculous now. Thea therefore tried hard to put unpleasant thoughts from her mind, being determined to enjoy the day.

Mabel and Francis decided that they would rebuild the waterfall by the summer house, and Thea helped them. The sun was warm enough for lunch in the garden, sitting in a sheltered hollow away from the wind. Thea managed to go through the whole day by avoiding calling Francis anything.

She couldn't call him Papa; the name just stuck in her throat, but she knew it would offend him if she called him Francis or Mr Hooper.

When it came to bedtime, Mabel produced a night-light which stood in a white porcelain stand. "Thought a little glow might help if you want to get out of bed," she said.

Thea was grateful for the light, but when she came to turn the wireless off she kept the ear phones in position so that any sound would be muffled. It was just getting light when she woke and wondered what was fixed to her head. Taking them off she placed them on the table, turned over and fell soundly asleep again.

On Sunday afternoon she returned home, and running down the common in the sunlight she felt quite happy. The weekend had gone better than she could ever have dreamt it would, for Mabel had been full of consideration and Mr Hooper kind. Aunty Mary was preparing tea when she walked into the dining room, Joy had gone for a walk with her father and Jean hadn't returned from Sunday school.

"Well, how have things gone?" Mary enquired.

"Fine," replied Thea. "They were very nice to me. Do you know, Aunty Mary, Mr Hooper gave me a wireless."

Aunty Mary sniffed disapprovingly and said, "How silly."

Thea longed to say it wasn't a bit silly, but she thought better of it. "He wants me to call him Papa," she said, "but I can't do that."

Mary looked at her and Thea noticed how tense and upset she looked. "They are trying to woo you. I knew they would," she said hoarsely. "They will do everything to get you away from me."

Thea was stunned. "No," she said, "I'm staying with you."

"For how long?" Mary was on the verge of tears. "I know they will work it."

At this point Robert came in through the front door and into the dining room. "What's the matter, May?" he said, using his pet name for her. "What has upset you?"

Tears glistened in Mary's dark eyes. "They want to take her from me," she said. "He has already given her a wireless. They will try all sorts of things to persuade her."

Thea stood against the table fiddling with the lace edging of the cloth, not knowing what to say.

"Mabel is her mother," said Robert soothingly, putting his arm round Mary, "so she has every right."

"What right?" Mary pulled away from Robert. "She has no right. She gave birth to the child, but she hasn't bothered with her since. Who has looked after her, taught her, cared for her?"

"Come on Mary, don't upset yourself," said Robert. "Things haven't been discussed."

"I'm staying here," said Thea, feeling that she ought to say something, as she was the object of Mary's distress. She felt always that wherever she went or whatever she did she caused consternation. Other people just went on leading ordinary lives, and their actions were not the subject for debate or subterfuge.

"They seem happy with each other. I'm sure they don't want me," she said, but she felt deeply inside herself that they did, but she couldn't think why. She also knew that the matter would not be discussed with her, for whatever the grown-ups decided between themselves, her life would be influenced by their decision.

Most families had members away in the armed forces and the bombing of the cities was throwing a gloom over everyone's lives. Although the sirens sounded when the enemy aircraft droned overhead, very few bombs had fallen in the area, and those that had had been dropped by mistake. Several aircraft had been fetched down by the guns, with great excitement being aroused when the prisoners were captured.

One day when Thea was returning home from school, a German aircraft was spotted flying low over the tree tops. It was so low that the pilot could be seen in the cockpit and swastikas showed clearly on the sides. Thea and her friends crouched in a ditch watching it pass. They heard machine-gun fire, and were tense with the excitement of it all when they reached their homes.

Aunty Mary was almost hysterical with worry, for she had seen the thing fly over, and she knew that the children would be coming out of school. She dragged Thea indoors and kissed her with relief. She paced round like a caged demented lioness until Jean arrived through the gate, full of what she had seen and how many Germans she had spotted in the cockpit.

They heard rumours later that the aircraft had been machine-gunning people in the streets of Worcester, and that some people had been hit as they came out of the munitions factory. Several bombs had fallen on the outskirts of the town, but they were dropped from wounded aircraft attempting to make their way back across the Channel.

The family had agreed to spend the Christmas period with Mabel and Francis. It was their first Christmas together, so they were keen to have the family with them. Several chickens had been set aside and fattened on household scraps ready for the festive feast.

Francis knew someone who was killing a pig—quite illegally— and a piece of pork had been promised to him. So great was the need for food that money and influence were bound to talk, and the black market flourished.

When Thea undid the parcel from her godmother, she found a large box of paints, a selection of brushes and several interesting books. There was also an invitation to a party which was being held in the country house where her godmother was living during the war.

"I doubt if you will be allowed to go," warned Mary.

"Allowed to go!" Thea was perplexed. "Who will stop me?"

"Francis," said Mary simply. "He wants all ties with that family severed."

"Why?" Thea couldn't understand.

"Because they are all part of your mother's past. He wants everything forgotten. He wants your mother to start life afresh without any connections with the past."

"But she is my godmother," Thea stammered.

"Yes, I know, but there it is; it is his wish," replied Mary. "You have to go by his wishes."

Obviously Mabel had written to Thea's godmother, for on the Sunday before Christmas, when Thea was with Mabel and Francis, her godmother arrived by chauffeur-driven car. Comment was of course passed on how she managed to keep a chauffeur or a car, but nevertheless that is how she arrived, and she alighted from the car looking as elegant as ever.

Francis was charming to her, invited her in, gave her sherry, but explained quite firmly that he wished connections to be severed. She felt that she ought to be allowed to see Thea on the odd occasions, although she understood his point of view. Francis agreed to the odd visit, but parties and social gatherings were most definitely to be a thing of the past and he felt that his wife should have no connection whatsoever with the family.

Thea felt that more and more she was coming under the domination of Francis, that his wishes were paramount. She didn't dislike him, but in a strange way she was afraid of him. He could be overwhelmingly charming, but on the other hand he could be extremely bad tempered and horrible if he didn't get his own way. Most people, Mabel included, gave in to him, as life was so much more pleasant when he was in an affable mood.

Thea couldn't help but think how strange life was. Last Christmas Francis and Emma were man and wife, continuing their life as they had done for the past twenty odd years, and now Emma was dead, Francis married to her mother and a family Christmas was being spent at the large, lonely house on the hill.

She thought of the previous Christmasses and the warm intimacies of her Aunt's and Uncle's house, and the unassuming presence of her grandmother.

Francis was a stranger, even though they had visited him and his wife on several occasions, but now he had become part of the family and a very dominant part too. Thea mused at the oddness of what had happened, and how a thunderstorm on a warm afternoon had altered the direction of her life.

Chapter Ten

THE winter was wickedly savage, which added to the burden of people's lives. Food was short, queues long and coal difficult to obtain. The wind howled with penetrating violence for weeks on end, seeming to jeer at the suffering.

Thea and Jean, together with the other children, struggled to school with the snow frequently filling their wellingtons. In the evening after trudging back in the bone-splintering cold, they would huddle round the fire in the kitchen and try to thaw out. Because of the shortage of fuel, there could only be one fire in the house, so the kitchen fire was the obvious choice as it heated the water as well as heating the oven.

Uncle Robert, too old to be called up, joined the A.R.P. and the St John Ambulance, so did his bit for the war effort when he had finished his day's work. Francis stayed at home nursing his ill-health, but as he was in his fifties, no one concerned themselves with requiring his services.

It was towards the end of February that Granny died. Her death happened suddenly and unexpectedly. She seemed to fade away, catching her family unawares.

Her funeral was held on a raw February morning in the church where she had worshipped for years. She was to be buried in the same grave as her husband, at the spot where Thea had helped to arrange the flowers so many times. The family stood grouped in the little church wrapped in combined grief, and when they filed behind the coffin on the way to the graveyard, the grey sky and the cold moisture-laden wind seemed to heighten the sadness of the occasion.

The big pile of earth against the grave, looking red and slimy because of the recent bad weather, made the flowers on the wreaths stand out in waxy brilliance. Most of the flowers were chrysanthemums, yellow, bronze and red, but Thea's spray of freesias lay apart like a touch of spring in the midst of the desolation. Mary had thought that Thea was being difficult when she had insisted on freesias instead of the traditional winter wreath, and would not listen when she said that Granny disliked chrysanthemums.

She could hear the vicar's voice, and from the corner of her eye she could see the wind blowing his surplice. Much to her surprise a little earth was sprinkled on the coffin after it had been lowered, and the vicar picked up the spray of freesias and threw them down on the coffin. Looking delicate and out of place they lay over the brass plate that bore the name Louise Mary.

During 1942 a large workforce was drafted into the town from the Ministry of Defence, and accommodation was at a premium. The position was made worse as many people had been seeking refuge from the bombing, so all spare houses and flats had been taken. The Authorities therefore decided that anyone who had spare bedrooms must be enforced to put people up. Francis and Mabel were told that they must accommodate eight people; it would have been ten had they not said that Thea was living with them. Margaret agreed to have three people, and Mary another two evacuees.

Francis and Mabel, suddenly faced with a complete upheaval of their ordered way of life, asked if they could accommodate men rather than a family. The thought of having women and children in the house was quite unbearable and they were thrown into panic at the possibility of such a thing. In the end Mabel agreed to have the ration books and prepare an evening meal for the men, rather than have them messing round the kitchen, warming themselves soup or making toast. She would allow them the use of a sitting room cum dining room, one of the bathrooms and their allocated bedrooms. In this way she felt that perhaps they would be able to retain a little privacy.

Thea was told that she would have to go and live with her mother and stepfather as the only domestic help they could get was from an elderly lady who lived nearby, so another pair of hands would be badly needed. Mary had prepared herself, since her sister's marriage, for the fact that she would lose Thea, when the shock came she took it stoically. Joy had recently started school, so Mary spent quite a lot of her day going backwards and forwards to the school, and trying to adjust her daughter to the strange scholastic environment.

Thea was not consulted, she was merely told. She could do little else but resign herself to the inevitable. When informed that she would be required to help with the domestic arrangements, she was quite disconcerted, for peeling potatoes and mopping floors she really disliked. She loved school, her studies and her friends, she didn't want to be living in the big house away from all she loved. However she was forced to conform to the wants of Mabel and Francis.

Thea began to call Francis, Pop, as a compromise for papa, which she just couldn't say. His moods were very unpredictable, as some days he could be happy and light-hearted, while other days a black gloom seemed to sit on him making him unbearable to be near. He pottered around the garden and, with the help of a pensioner from the village, managed to keep the garden in some form of control. Huge quantities of vegetables were grown, and the fruit trees were wonderfully fertile, producing plenty for bottling and jam-making.

Thea was expected to peel potatoes, dice carrots, chop cabbage, peel apples and generally get the vegetables ready for the evening meal. She would plead that her school work needed doing, but the pressing need was to get the meal ready for when the men returned from work in the evening. Her hands soon became sore and stained, and her school work began to suffer.

Some mornings she found it very difficult to get out of bed and put her mind to school work when her body wanted desperately to sleep. Often she felt very tired at school, so much so that her teacher passed comments about her lassitude, suggesting that perhaps a tonic was needed. When she noticed Thea's stained and grubby hands, she got quite cross with her telling her that "ladies" always kept their hands clean with their nails nicely manicured.

The men who had accommodation in the house were excellent company, being young, light-hearted post-graduates. They did justice to Mabel's cooking, consuming her soups and casseroles with great relish. Rabbits were easily available to supplement the meagre ration together with chickens which could be bartered for fruit and vegetables.

Thea carried in the tureens laden with food, frequently staying behind to chat to the young men. They often helped with the washing up, fooling and joking while it was being done. Francis, however, didn't always welcome their help; unless he was in a very good mood he preferred them to stay in their own room.

One of the young men, Chris Birch by name, would frequently help Thea with her maths when all the clearing up was done. He had a sister who was much the same age as Thea, so he had sympathy for her.

"You must work hard, Thea, and never neglect your school work," he said to her one evening. "Anything can be achieved if you really aim for it."

Thea told him that she wanted to be a doctor, but Francis had overheard the conversation and when she went back into the kitchen he was very cross with her.

"What do you mean?" he asked. "How can you be a doctor? You aren't going to stay on at school."

Thea looked at him, noticing how dark and angry his face was. "I am," she said. "I am going to be a doctor."

"You will not be staying on at school. I am responsible for you now. I have to pay all the bills. I can't afford to have you at school and, what's more, you are needed here. Your duty is to be here, helping your mother."

"Duty!" Thea muttered under her breath, with her eyes stinging with tears. "What duty?"

"Stop muttering!" demanded Francis. "Also I don't like the way you keep talking to those young men."

Thea went to her room, weary with housework, doubting if she could ever achieve anything in the face of such opposition.

One Saturday morning when she had planned to sit in the garden preparing essays for school, her well planned scheme was shattered by Francis asking her to wash over both kitchen floors, after which she was to get the shopping from the village. The shopping had been ordered, but only one delivery was allowed a week by van because of the petrol shortage.

Thea protested, explaining how she wanted to do her essays, but Francis told her that they would have to wait because it was important that she help her expectant mother. Thea gasped at the news disbelieving that Mabel and Francis could have a baby at their age.

Mabel who was sitting at the kitchen table sipping coffee and reading the morning paper, looked up, smiled weakly, and said, "Yes, Thea. How do you fancy a baby brother? Pop wants a son, so I am sure that is what it is going to be."

Thea didn't know what to say for she was speechless with surprise, but she managed to smile and mutter a response which gave a suggestion of pleasure. She found a bucket, filled it with hot, soapy water and began to mop the floor, her mind a flurry of thoughts. She was disappointed with herself that she couldn't feel pleased, but somehow it just didn't seem right that her mother and Francis should have a baby.

Later Francis said to her, "Your mother will have to rest a great deal, so you will have to help all you can."

Thea felt quite defeated for she knew that she did help as much as she could. Everything that she wanted to do was of secondary importance, and with Mabel expecting a baby her position would be even worse, as she would be required to do more and more.

Later in the morning, as she was dragging the heavy baskets of shopping up the steep slope from the shops, she felt that the future looked black and a feeling verging on hatred for Francis burnt within her.

The next day she visited Aunty Mary as she had done most Sundays since going to live with Mabel and Francis. She liked to go to Sunday school and see her old friends from the village. Mabel and Francis usually spent a quiet day on Sundays as the young men were not around, so an evening meal was not required. If the weather was fine she would walk all of the way, but if wet she took a bus which halved the journey.

This particular Sunday was fine and sunny, so Thea walked across the golf course, then down the common to her old home. Mary was setting the tea in the dining room as Thea arrived. It was her usual practice to lay the table for tea straight after clearing away the dinner things, then all she had to do when it was time for tea was bring out the food. Robert was sitting in his usual armchair in the sitting room, with his eyes closed and his pipe held loosely in his hands. Jean was getting ready for Sunday school and Joy was playing in her toy cupboard.

"Hello, darling," said Mary as Thea entered the room.

Thea walked across, kissed her aunt, and said suddenly, as though she must relieve herself of the dreadful tidings, "Mum's expecting a baby."

Aunty Mary's face expressed consternation and surprise. "What did you say?" It was as though she couldn't believe what her niece had said. "Thea, what did you say?" she said again.

"Mum's expecting," exclaimed Thea, aware that her news was of paramount importance to her aunt.

"Did you hear that, Robert?" called Mary, putting down the pile of cups and saucers that she had in her hand and walking into the sitting room.

Thea followed and saw Robert open a sleepy, watery eye and say, "Bit risky I should have thought."

"Risky is putting it very mildly. Absolutely ridiculous I call it," said Mary with force. "She is far too old for starting a family."

"I've got to do a lot of extra things to help," said Thea. "I have to wash the floors, get the shopping, help get the dinner, wash it up!" She stood back to see if she would get any sympathy.

Mary shook her head sadly, looked at Thea a long, long look. "I'm sorry, I really am. I can do nothing. I only wish I could."

"I don't want to stay there." Thea's eyes began to fill with tears. "I want to stay with you."

Mary, putting her arm gently round Thea, said, "Never mind; things will work out all right in the end, but you will have to stay there. I can't help."

The tears began to flow freely and Thea sobbed, "I don't like housework. I don't like that horrible big house."

"Now come on, darling, don't upset yourself," said Mary. "You must be grown up about it all."

Robert began to scrape his pipe out thoughtfully into the ashtray. He was a man of few words who viewed life very seriously. Looking at Thea he asked kindly, "Are you keeping up with your school work?"

"No, how can I?" came the tearful reply. "It's very difficult with so much housework to do."

"Can't you talk to them or sort the situation out?" asked Robert. He sucked the stem of his empty pipe and looked questioningly at Mary. "It's not right, you know, to stop her studying."

"Oh Robert!" said Mary in an exasperated voice. "How can I help? Talking will only make the matter worse, I feel."

"Mrs Todd said my hands are a disgrace," wailed Thea. "Look at them!" She held her hands towards her aunt.

Jean came running downstairs. "What's up?" she demanded with her usual frankness.

"She is upset," said Mary. Then turning towards Thea, "I will get you some gloves," she added.

"I don't like washing floors," said Thea looking at Jean, but instead of sympathy a sparkle came into Jean's eyes and a smile played round her lips.

"Are you crying because of that? I don't mind washing floors. I'll wash the floors," she said.

Thea wiped her eyes with the back of her hand thanking Jean at the same time for her generous offer. She couldn't explain to Jean that it wasn't just the floors, it was everything that seemed to batter and defeat her. It was losing her identity. It was the everlasting struggle for recognition. It was always having to take second place and being of no value.

"Now, isn't that kind?" said Mary. "If Jean could help you sometimes it may not seem so bad. Now wash your face, then off you go to Sunday school." She smiled at her niece kindly. "I'll have something really nice for tea."

Walking towards the Institute with Jean, Thea began to feel less stressed. Everything around was known, friendly, safe and sure. The cottage gardens bright with summer flowers breathed reassurance, as did the passive, contented sheep lying in the shade under the lime trees.

In the Institute the smell of dusty wood, aged hymn books and the harsh smell of Jeyes fluid from the toilets added to make the warm, familiar, friendly aroma of Sunday school. Generous, kind Mr Hughes, full of patience and wisdom, and Miss Gittings thumping out the familiar tunes on the rather worn-out piano helped Thea to view life again from a gentler aspect.

The months passed by. Between home and school Thea carried out her existence. She tried to keep her enthusiasm for school work and wrote her essays in the still loneliness of early dawn. Jean was a frequent visitor on Saturdays, helping cheerfully with the chores, making Francis laugh quite frequently at her direct and witty good humour. She often stayed the night, sleeping with Thea in her room.

There was so much noise generally in the house that footsteps in the night could belong to anyone, but Thea was still convinced that the house was haunted. Jean would laugh and say that she didn't hear anything; if she did it was only someone going to the bathroom. Aunty Margaret, however, heard footsteps clearly when she slept in Thea's room, but she was sure that they wouldn't do any harm, as they were the steps of some poor, restless soul.

To be on the safe side, however, she helped Thea drag the chest of drawers, placing it against the door that led to the passage where the sound came from. Francis was cross, snorting his disapproval, but the chest of drawers stayed in the new position, easing Thea's mind.

One cold morning Francis woke Thea before her usual alarm clock did. "Your mother isn't well," he said. "She is in awful pain."

Thea sat up, feeling only half awake, and struggled to focus her eyes on Francis, standing by the bed looking pale and worried. "Mum, did you say? Ill, did you say?"

"Yes. Get dressed," whispered Francis in an agitated voice. "Go and get Mrs Mac. She might know if it's anything serious."

Mrs Mac had been a midwife, only giving up her calling as the war broke out. She had delivered countless babies and her skill and wisdom were still respected in the area. She lived in a cottage a few hundred yards up the lane and had been a friend of Francis's and Emma's for many years.

Thea jumped out of bed, pulled on her jumper and skirt, pushed her feet into her shoes and moved towards the stairs. As she passed Mabel's room she heard a low, agonized moan which sent her running down the stairs, out through the front door and along the driveway in the direction of Mrs Mac's cottage. It was only when she was outside that she realized how cold it was, the keen wind hitting her like a clout round the face. It was quite dark with stars in the sky, so that she had to grope her way up the bank that led to Mrs Mac's gate.

She was wondering how on earth she was going to wake the old lady, when the wind wrenched the gate from her grasp, flinging it to with force. Mrs Mac, being conditioned over the years to gates being flung open in the night by agitated fathers, was out of bed peering through the window before Thea had reached the door.

Opening her casement window, she called out into the darkness, "Who is it?"

"Mrs Hooper is ill," said Thea. "Mr Hooper said could you please come."

"Has he sent for the doctor?" enquired the old midwife. "Anyhow, tell him I'll get dressed and come."

"I'll wait for you," called Thea. "I'll guide you back." She stood on the doorstep shivering because, apart from guiding Mrs Mac back, she was afraid to go back into the house with her mother moaning in pain.

Mrs Mac opened the door. "Come inside," she said. "I won't take long getting dressed." She was wrapped in her late husband's check woollen dressing gown with her grey plaits hanging down her back.

Thea stood in the little cluttered sitting room shivering with cold. A black cat lay asleep on one of the chairs and he looked disapprovingly at being disturbed at such an early hour, curling himself even tighter by placing his head beneath his paws. The room was filled with the treasures of a lifetime giving the appearance that nothing was ever thrown away.

As they walked back to the house together, this time guided by Mrs Mac's torch, she said, "If she is in labour, there will be no chance of saving the baby as it's much too early."

Thea hadn't thought about Mabel having the baby just yet and, as for losing the baby, the thought had never crossed her mind. Francis was so certain that he would have a son, making marvellous plans for the future, that Thea had never doubted that things would turn out well.

"Twelve more weeks," said Mrs Mac, making noises of doom with her teeth. "That's too long. It can't live."

Mrs Mac went upstairs, leaving Thea sitting miserably in the kitchen wondering what she should do. She could hear voices upstairs mingled with the moaning sound. Picking up the poker she raked out the ashes from the grate and began to relight the fire. There were plenty of dry sticks by the side of the oven, so a fire could soon be started which would warm up the kitchen, at least. As she was preparing the sticks she heard Francis run downstairs to the phone.

"Can you come straight away, please?" he said, his voice sounding tense and dreadful. He was ringing the doctor, even though it was so early, indicating that things were very serious. As he passed the kitchen door, he stopped, looked at Thea lighting the fire and said, "Your mother is really bad. Can you tell the boys to be quiet when they are getting ready?"

Thea didn't know what to say, but he had gone before she could think of a reply. Chris Birch, awakened by the disturbance, came into the kitchen and asked what the trouble was.

"Mum's ill," said Thea striking a match. "The doctor is coming."

"Is it the baby?" enquired Chris anxiously.

The flame licked the newspaper, catching the sticks, making the grate glow brightly. "I don't really know," said Thea, "but I think that's what it is."

"It's ages yet," said Chris, whistling through his teeth. "That's bad, really bad." He filled the large kettle, placed it on the cooker and arranged the cups on the kitchen table.

Thea put small pieces of coal on to the burning wood, getting a little warmth from the flames. She was glad of Chris's company even though they said little for somehow it seemed inappropriate to talk. The doctor arrived just as the kettle boiled. Francis, on hearing his car, had run down to let him in. Chris made two pots of tea, taking one upstairs for his companions and leaving the other on the kitchen table.

It seemed an age that they sat in silence sipping tea before the doctor came downstairs to the telephone, so breaking the awful suspense. Before going back upstairs he put his head round the kitchen door, informing them that he had ordered an ambulance to take Mrs Hooper into hospital.

"How is she?" Chris called after his disappearing body.

The doctor stopped and went back into the kitchen. "Mrs Hooper will be all right," he whispered. "She needs a good rest, but the baby was still-born. Great pity, but one of those awful quirks of nature, sending him out in to the world too soon."

Chris asked him if he would like a cup of tea—it seemed the only thing to say in the circumstances—but the doctor said that he would go back upstairs, but that a cup of tea would be most welcome after Mrs Hooper had gone to hospital. Thea and Chris sat looking at each other in shocked silence, knowing what devastating anguish of loss would be going on upstairs and both feeling unsure of what to say, never having faced such a situation before.

After the ambulance had gone, Thea, having made a fresh pot of tea, took the tray into the drawing room. She dreaded having to face Francis as she knew his grief would be inconsolable. She watched apprehensively from the window as he, the doctor and Mrs Mac, forming a small group, chatted in the driveway. As they turned to walk up the front steps Francis's drawn, anguished face became visible, confirming her worst fears.

As he entered the room Francis burst into floods of tears. He flung himself on to the sofa, buried his face into a velvet cushion, while his body shook with sobs. Mrs Mac began to pour out the tea in a quiet, matter-of-fact manner, while Thea stood by the window overcome with embarrassment and disbelief.

"It's just reaction," said the doctor quietly to Thea. "It's been a dreadful shock for him." Picking up his cup of tea he walked towards the window to stand by Thea. "Don't worry, Mrs Hooper has just gone into hospital for a rest. She will be quite well again in a few weeks."

Francis began pounding his fist into the cushion. "It's so unfair, so unfair," he sobbed. "All my life I have wanted a son—then I had one, only to have him snatched away from me—it's most unfair. Oh God! I must be the most unlucky creature that was ever born. Why did it have to happen? Oh God!"

"Come on, old chap," murmured the doctor. "I know it's awful, but these things do happen."

"Always to me," wailed the demented Francis. "Always to me. God must hate me." He rolled his face miserably round the cushion, thumping the settee at the same time.

"There will be another time," soothed Mrs Mac. "Next time lucky."

The doctor gave Mrs Mac a quizzical look, raising his eyebrow and pursing his lips at the same time. Walking across to Francis, he patted him on the shoulder. "Come along, Mr Hooper, think of your wife," he said. "You have to help her get over the loss of her baby, because it is not going to be easy for her."

Francis, raising bloodshot eyes to the doctor, choked, "Not easy for my wife? How do you think it is for me?"

The doctor sat on the window seat drinking his tea quietly, for he knew it was no good talking to Francis as he was beyond reasoning with. He passed the odd comment to Thea and Mrs Mac, then slipped away as he had other patients to attend to.

Thea didn't go to school that day and she was glad that Mrs Mac stayed to help her clear up, as well as helping her to cope with the distraught Francis. Nellie from the village arrived to do her usual chores and, seeing what the situation was, she agreed to increase her hours doing whatever she felt was necessary.

During the next few weeks Francis gradually got over his loss but he was depressed and taciturn, cursing providence for what he believed was solely his loss. In a way he blamed Mabel for losing his baby, constantly reminding her of the fact that she lost the baby because she didn't rest sufficiently. Mabel was listless and apathetic, seeming to have little interest in anything, which at times caused tremendous tensions between herself and Francis.

"It's not my fault that I had a premature birth," she would shriek at him. "I am too old for babies, that's why I lost it."

His defence mechanism would be to fly into a rage, stomp upstairs and lock himself in his bedroom for hours on end.

One Sunday morning when Thea was in the drawing room preparing some work for school, she looked towards Mabel who was sitting in the window seat gazing into the valley, and she noticed how tired and sad she looked. Her figure had thickened, her previously beautifully styled hair was no longer so, and her hands were swollen so that the rings on her fingers dug into her flesh. The smart, elegant woman had vanished and a sad middle-aged person now gazed through the window with a look of contained longing.

Thea could never remember feeling sorry for Mabel, but she did so then. "Do you wish you hadn't married Francis?" she said suddenly.

Mabel glanced at her with an expression of surprise on her face, then continued to stare through the window, not answering for several moments. "I gave up my freedom. Freedom is something to treasure," she said. "I never realised what it would be like to lose my freedom."

Thea didn't know how to answer for she felt that if anyone had given up freedom it was herself, only she hadn't given it up, she had

had it taken away from her, so she was puzzled by her mother's words.

"You love Francis though, don't you?" she replied.

Mabel shrugged her shoulders, "I suppose so, whatever love means," she said. "Francis can be very pleasant company, but he never takes me out. He is obsessed with the idea of having a son which I don't like. Also I feel that he uses me."

"Don't stay with him then," said Thea simply, not really comprehending the complexity of her statement.

"Oh, don't be silly," retorted Mabel, "I have given up everything to marry Francis. I have got to stay with him and make the most of it."

"Do you like this house?" asked Thea, trying to change the subject. "I don't because it's spooky."

"Of course it's not spooky," replied Mabel irritably, "but it's too big. A place like this needs several full-time staff, otherwise it gets out of hand." She sighed and tried to make an effort to push her hair into shape. "I should like a cottage with a manageable garden, so that I would be able to sit in the sun."

Thea wished that she could tell Mabel how she felt, but she was unable to express her feelings; instead she kept all her emotions locked within her. Sucking the end of her pen, she thought how much she disliked her own position of having to live with Mabel and Francis. She brooded too on the awful possibility of having to leave school at fourteen and so say farewell to all her hopes and aspirations. She wished that she had the courage to stand up and shriek, "Look what you have done to me!", but instead she said nothing, keeping quiet because deeply embedded within her was a feeling of loyalty mixed with pity for her mother.

During the summer-time one of the young men left to get married and a Mr Walters took his place. He was a middle-aged family man from Wolverhampton who was planning to buy a house in the area for his wife and daughters, but in the meantime, as his work required him to be in the area, he took rooms with Francis and Mabel. He was such a pleasant, friendly man, that Mabel and Francis took an instant liking to him, so that in a very short time he was eating his meals with them and spending most of his evenings in their company. His presence was like a breath of fresh air in the house for he was marvellously good fun to be with. He would tell them anecdotes from his past, amusing stories that had happened at work and lovely accounts of his family's life. He would talk to Francis as they walked in the grounds, or sat around the log fire contentedly smoking their pipes. With Mr Walters, Francis was at ease, rarely getting irritable when he was around.

As Mr Walters wanted to bring his wife and family to live in the area, Mabel invited them to stay so that they could familiarise themselves with the locality and so choose where they wanted to buy a house. One daughter was the same age as Thea, but the other one was nine years older. The older girl, because of her interests and commitments in Wolverhampton, declined to stay, but the younger girl, whose name was Patricia, was delighted to go away with her parents and explore the area where their new home was likely to be.

A general rearrangement was made upstairs, and the young man who roomed with Mr Walters agreed to move out and share with one of the others, so that Mrs Walters could have his bed. It was decided that Patricia should sleep in Thea's room, and that they would all eat together as friends.

From the first moment that they were introduced to each other Thea and Pat became firm friends. Pat was a pretty girl, with a lively, vivacious personality, sparkling dark eyes and a lovely fresh complexion. She seemed full of spontaneous joy and self–confidence which made Thea admire her instantly.

Her wardrobe was extensive because her mother was clever at dress–making with a flair for making pretty teenage clothes. Pat had such a happy, friendly nature, although in no way conceited; in fact she flung compliments around like confetti expecting nothing back in return.

Mrs Walters' direct friendliness and good humour appealed to Mabel and she began to laugh in her company as she had not laughed for months. It was impossible to feel depressed in Mrs Walters' presence for her good humour was contagious.

Mabel told Mrs Walters about the loss of her baby and of her husband's desire for a son. She also told her that she was afraid of attempting another pregnancy because of her age, but that she was in a dilemma as she wanted to please her husband.

Mrs Walters' advice was direct and uncomplicated as she felt that Mabel should in no way consider having another baby. "You must not put your life at risk. You have tried but nature decided otherwise ," she told Mabel. "Now be content in each other's company and put all thoughts of babies out of your mind."

Mabel, sitting with Mrs Walters on the terrace in the sunshine, thought how easy it was for her, as she had such a wise, sensible husband who didn't bother about sons, as he was contented with his two lovely daughters, whereas Francis considered that he was lacking in some fundamental way because he hadn't got a son to follow him.

"Take pleasure in each other's company," suggested Mrs Walters. "Do things together. You've got Thea; take pleasure in seeing her grow up."

Mabel looked at her new friend's sparkling eyes, her elegant clothes and smart hair-style and realized that she had let herself go both physically and mentally.

"I am sure you are right. I only wish I had your self-confidence," said Mabel. "Look at me. I have gone so plump that none of my clothes fit properly."

Mrs Walters boosted her morale by offering to alter some of her clothes and perming her hair. This offer helped Mabel's self-esteem tremendously, simply because a friend was prepared to put herself out for her. It was friendship that Mabel had missed so much since her marriage to Francis, so she appreciated the closeness of Mrs Walters very much.

The Walters spent a number of family, house-hunting holidays with Mabel and Francis before finally deciding on the area and the house that they wanted to live in. Each holiday the friendships deepened with the affection between the two families becoming stronger. It was a foregone conclusion that when the Walters were finally settled they would remain close friends with the Hoopers.

Mr Walters would often chat to Thea in a fatherly way. He understood Thea's situation and although sympathetic with her was loath to cause any friction in the family. When Thea told him that she wanted to stay on at school but that her stepfather wouldn't allow her to, he encouraged her not to be down-hearted but to look to the future, as there would be plenty of opportunities then.

"Sometimes," he said, "we are faced with a situation that cannot at the time be altered, so what we have to do is alter our attitude to the situation. Your mother needs you at the moment. At a later date you can finish your education and do everything that you want to do."

Thea was not totally convinced but she knew that her situation couldn't be altered and she appreciated his kindly advice. She felt that she would be trapped for a number of years and then it would be difficult to resume her studies.

One day Thea and her friends were sitting under the old walnut tree in the garden. They had been picking the nuts up from the sun-dried grass and their fingers were stained a light brown. The basket containing the nuts lay in the grass, all appearing the same golden, late summery colour. There was Pat, Iris, Mavis, Jean and cousin Loretta who had come to stay. Loretta had grown tall and willowy with fair hair, intense grey eyes and a most extensive vocabulary which quite startled the other girls. She was doing very well at grammar school and it would seem that the world lay at her feet.

Mavis had grown tall, far outstripping Thea. She was bronzed, sporty, intelligent, aiming as she had always done for a career in science. Jean, who asked little of life but gave plenty through her cheerful, uncomplaining disposition, knew that as soon as she reached her fourteenth birthday she must return to Birmingham to help her mother support her younger brother and sister. Her father had died suddenly with cancer, leaving their mother in very difficult circumstances. Jean accepted her position completely, knowing exactly where her duty lay, never questioning the fact that she must help her family. Iris, petite, brown-haired, hazel-eyed, was the same quiet, gentle girl that she had been when younger. She had no desire to stay at school and was longing for the day when she could be released from the boredom of the classroom. She told the girls that she would like to work in a library or bookshop, but she didn't want to study further at the moment.

Thea lay in the grass on her back looking up at the odd puffs of cloud floating in the endless sea of sky. She pulled at the golden, ripe grasses that sprouted around her head and listened to the conversation of her friends. She was the only one that was being forced to do something against her wishes. "I can't do what I want to do," she said. "I've got to leave school when I'm fourteen and stay here."

"I wouldn't mind staying here," said Jean. "I think your idea of being a doctor is daft anyway. Who wants to muck around with people's rotten bodies?"

Thea didn't answer for there was nothing she could really say. How could she explain that she wanted to do just that? Jean was always so uncomplicated that she envied her.

"I'm going to have a shop," announced Pat.

Thea sat up and looked at her. "A shop?" she said. "How?"

Pat smiled. "Not straight away, silly. When I leave school I shall get a job in someone else's shop and learn the business of buying and selling. When I have learnt how to manage a shop I shall have my own and sell beautiful clothes."

The girls sat bathed in sunlight absorbing what Pat had said. In each young head were different hopes, dreams and aspirations, but each girl had to come to terms with her own limitations and family situations and yet look towards the future with enthusiasm.

Mavis, always serious, dignified and wise beyond her years, said, "I wonder what we shall all be doing in ten years' time. I wonder if we shall have achieved our aims in life. Whatever we do though, we must always remain friends."

Thea lay back in the grass encased in its somnambulant warmth. The girls' voices floated over her in soft waves. It occurred to her that in ten years time she would be twenty three; an age so far into the future that it seemed beyond reach. She wondered whether at twenty three one was too old to have hopes and ambitions, but instead just accepted life as it was. With a deep rooted certainty she knew that she would always keep contact with her friends as they were such a valuable part of her life that she couldn't envisage her existence without them, so she agreed wholeheartedly with Mavis's sentiments. She wished that she could sometimes see into the future, just a little, and have some idea of the way her life would go.

Rolling onto her stomach she looked through the striped, summer grasses at the confident, bronzed face of Mavis. "If I have to leave school next year, Mavis, how can I continue to learn?" she asked.

Mavis looked serious and screwed up her forehead in earnest contemplation. "I think you can go to 'Night School' at the College, she said. "They give you lessons, and essays to write, and suggest the books that you need to read."

Thea turned the information slowly over in her mind, wondering if she would be allowed to go to Night School, especially if the classes were held late in the evening.

"Do you ever wish," said Iris suddenly, "that everything would stop and that we could all stay as we are, just sitting here together under this tree, for ever and ever?"

Pat appeared to wince at Iris's remark, for she was very much a girl who was looking enthusiastically at the future and was therefore anxious to get on with her life, but Mavis smiled and said, "Yes I often wish the world would stop, particularly when I'm really, really happy."

Thea broke off a stalk of golden grass and began to chew it contemplatively. She watched Jean trying to extract an unripe walnut from its shell, using as a digging tool a piece of wicker from the basket. As Jean put a piece of the white nut into her mouth she instantly contorted her face in disgust. "It's 'orrible," she said, "really 'orrible."

"You only have to eat them when they're brown and dry," volunteered Loretta. "Like everything else you must eat them at the right time!"

Thea thought of her cousin's words, realizing that this was so for everything in the world. There was a time to seek the first celandine in the woods; watch for the returning swallows; or pick the first juicy blackberries of summer. She put her face deeply in the grass, and the hot, dry, almost acrid smell of the grass roots struck her nostrils violently. Young as she was she knew that life went on, bounding down unknown pathways, regardless of human desires, and she couldn't help but think of kindly old Mr Hughes, when he would remark philosophically that, 'there is a time, and a purpose for all things under heaven'.

Cappella Archive
Limited Editions

Cappella Archive provides a similar mastering service for
the written word that a recording studio does for music.
The typeset book file is stored in a digitized Archive and
copies are printed on request as they are ordered; the
Archive behaving as the printing equivalent of audio or
video dubbing.

The Archive is independent of computer systems and
may be re-edited at any time or directly converted for
quantity production.